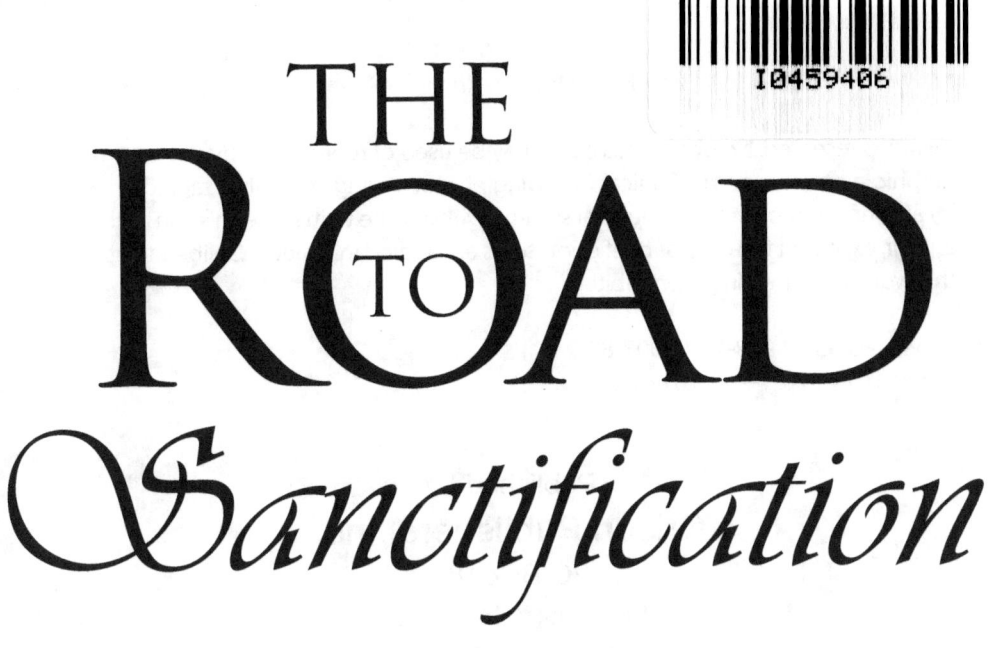

THE ROAD TO *Sanctification*

Where the Favor of
Spiritual Prosperity Awaits

SANDRA HARDISTER QUERIN
Foreword by Rev. John Burns

Paperback ISBN 978-1-960007-87-2
eBook ISBN 978-1-960007-88-9

Published by

Orison Publishers, Inc.

PO Box 188
Grantham, PA 17027
www.OrisonPublishers.com

Contents

Dedication

With a grateful heart, this little instruction manual
is dedicated to my precious friend, Pastor Dave Tanner,
who encouraged me to set this forth long ago,
just before he went on to Glory.

Foreword

As the Director of Central Valley Teen Challenge for the past ten years, I've had the privilege of knowing Rev. Sandi Querin through her leadership at Revival Center Church in Clovis and Abba's Heart Ministries in Kingsburg, California. Rev. Querin is a spiritually dynamic leader whose impact for Christ in the Central Valley is both profound and far-reaching. Her partnership with Central Valley Teen Challenge has been marked by compassion, conviction and a true shepherd's heart—serving the Lord and others with unrelenting love and spiritual power.

In *The Road to Sanctification*, Rev. Querin offers both challenge and encouragement to those seeking a deeper relationship with Jesus Christ. This book is a call to awaken—to become more attentive to the Spirit of God and to refocus our heart on eternal things. It reminds us that spiritual victory begins with purity of heart and that healing is available for the wounds that have shaped our soul.

Rev. Querin does not shy away from the realities of spiritual warfare. She exposes the tactics of the enemy and invites the reader to follow God's leading for victory. Through her words, we are led on a path of purification, consecration and sanctification—a journey that requires honesty, humility and surrender.

This book will challenge you to search your heart for anything that hinders spiritual growth, such as a victim mentality, unforgiveness, fear or misplaced identity. It offers hope for inner healing and restoration in the presence of God. It calls us to move forward from pain, to confront what holds us back, and to embrace the sacrifice required to serve the Lord wholeheartedly.

Rev. Querin writes with love and truth, guiding the reader toward personal reformation and spiritual renewal. Her message is clear:

spiritual growth is not for the faint of heart, but for those who are ready to go deeper with God. She walks alongside the reader, sharing from her own experience and pointing the way to new and incredible things the Lord desires to do in our life. Herein you will discover the last stronghold in your life and rejoice to find its end.

I wholeheartedly recommend *The Road to Sanctification* to every Christian who is serious about his or her spiritual journey. If you are ready to go to new places with God, this book will be a faithful companion.

Rev. John Burns, MS, CADC
Director, Central Valley Teen Challenge

Preface

Welcome to the world of God's design for your appointment with sanctification. Life is hard, no doubt about it. All that you have gone through and are rolling around in even now has a purpose. You are being built by the Master Builder. Only He can see the blueprint; He knows what He is doing.

He will not let go of you. He will take you through to the other side of this horrible valley. The Lord will help you to rise above it all for the purposes of the Cross of Calvary.

As with many of us, when we try to accomplish something wonderful, even powerful, for the Lord, every kind of tragedy comes upon us. The writing of this book was no different. My heart broke over and over again. I endured, just as you undoubtedly have done—sometimes limping, sometimes weeping and sometimes pushing. I hoped that the betrayal, loss, disease, pain and disappointment would end. But they did not. Not then.

It would take four decades of unrelenting horror before my deliverance would come. Jesus would hold me, and we would wait together. This book would whisper at me in the night: "God didn't tell you to write if you felt like it; He told you to write it." Sure, I wrote other things and I did other things. But this, would wait until now.

Here we stand with grief, maybe catastrophic grief, as our travel companion. Nevertheless, we go onward and forward, for we are not content at being grief-stricken. Let's not forget that while tragedy is on one side of the coin, Jesus is on the other. His desire is to own both sides of the coin, and that is the cause of this little book. As the saying goes, "All the bad stuff that could happen, already happened." So let's go!

―――――――――――――◆―――――――――――――

"The old cross slew men; the new cross entertains them. The old cross condemned; the new cross amuses. The old cross destroyed confidence in the flesh; the new cross encourages it."

—A.W. Tozer
The Divine Conquest, 1950

―――――――――――――◆―――――――――――――

Introduction

"A lot of people think that Christianity is you doing all the righteous things you hate and avoiding all the wicked things you love in order to go to Heaven. No, that's a lost man with religion. A Christian is a person whose heart has been changed; they have new affections."

—Paul Washer

The journey in these pages is about the pain of rebirth and the splendor of perseverance through affliction. It is about loss and gain, life and death, and all points in between. It is about Jesus, who fills the cracks of our soul, for it is through those cracks His light shines the brightest.

These pages will not pet your soul like a lost puppy and tell you that you will not encounter trials. Rather, they honestly tell you that you will encounter these things, that in your longest hours, when betrayal gives way to the dark night of your soul and loss takes your breath away...God is still your Eternal Father.

God waits to be heard, but He rarely is because we have become accustomed to looking right past Him, bound to our preconceived and supposed ideas. These ideas can hide the anger and fear that hold us back by guarding the wounds that keep us broken and in despair.

Worship the part of God that you know: find Jesus.

Pain and loss have a way of creating a wall that we didn't bargain for. Pain and loss have a way of making such a flesh-colored mark on our soul that we cannot tell it's there. We only see that mark when we try to cross over the pain and disappointment.

When we are forced to consider the option of sitting down, staying still and dealing with that pain and loss, then comes a scary hope, one that dares us to believe again. How do we take authority over our lost hopes and dreams, over dead promises that leave an image but have no voice?

So, we sit in the mess, drowning in our sorrow and unresolved trauma while the drama rages all around us. It is a move of the Holy Spirit that we need, and He is here to get the job done.

Taking ownership is different than having authority.

Come and see.

————————————◆————————————

"Down through the centuries, in times of trouble and trial God has brought courage to the hearts of those who love Him....You can look ahead with promise, hope, and joy."
—Billy Graham

————————————◆————————————

CHAPTER ONE

Summoned to Be Courageous

"Fear imprisons, faith liberates; fear paralyzes, faith empowers; fear disheartens, faith encourages; fear sickens, faith heals; fear makes useless, faith makes serviceable."
—Harry Emerson Fosdick

To be courageous takes a knowing. Courage stands on a foundation of bravery and fearlessness. If you don't think you can do a thing, then you probably can't. When you realize that the way for you to do that thing has already been paid for and secured, everything changes. When you realize that you *are* a signer on that account, almost immediately you start writing checks.

We cannot hope our way into this land; we must *know*. God has called us to plow in His field for His Kingdom, for souls and righteousness. Plow straight rows, my darling saint, plow straight rows.

What you hold to be true must be binding upon you, and this leaves no room for fence-sitting. *Bravery will allow you to hope for change while courage puts your soul into motion and your feet to work.*

At the end of the day, you cannot be worried about ruffling feathers, since you are going for plucking them out. That is what it takes to line up and be ready for the war against God's enemies.

Because of the shed blood of Jesus Christ, the victory that was measured at Calvary cancels the enemy's plans over our life. He has to leave every situation that concerns us.

1

Jesus rose from the dead; this is an immutable fact that the enemy cannot reconcile within his strategies against us. We together are His people, the sheep of His pasture. (See Psalm 100:3 and Revelation 12:11). We must know this!

The enemy's principalities and strongholds are void as we call upon the Lord. The enemy has already been overcome by the blood of the Lamb and by the power of the Word of God. A risen Savior is our very testimony. Our God has spoken the words of life, even abundant life, over us.

When we take our authority in the spirit, we will find that our enemy has already been overcome by the blood of Christ. (See John 16:33.) The enemy cannot cross that bloodline to get to us. In our authority within Jesus Christ, when we pray, we predominate every situation as ordained by God's provision stored in heaven for us and our situation. This includes every relationship and every opportunity that present themselves to us.

As we rest in the knowing of the pending answers, our soul begins to worship from the purest place and Christ Himself begins to enjoin the answers to our requests. No evil will be brought to bear upon us while we wait on our Lord because, when we yield to Him, He takes control.

The Word of God says that "my times are in your hands" (Psalm 31:15 NIV), which means we have just slid into home plate. We are deemed "safe." We just shake the dust off ourselves as we walk to the dugout and wait for the next inning.

Being still and waiting on a Hero with a proven track record is not a bad thing. It shouldn't be hard either, but I guess it depends on what you know about *Who* you know. (See Psalm 46:10.)

As we seek the Lord for His perfect will, the laws of the Kingdom of God come into play. It is in the seeking and the waiting where God's plans are easily revealed. They come alive as we wait, which affirms that the answers will come in the perfect timing of God Himself.

As we walk in the authority of knowing God's will with a contented and waiting heart, we are actually authorizing the receipt to be issued and the "goods" or answers to be delivered.

Wait on the One who is worth waiting on.

We are not to declare and decree, as some may say; rather, we are to wait patiently on Jesus and fall into a mature faith, which is trust. Psalm 40:1 (NIV) says, "I waited patiently for the Lord; he turned to me and heard my cry."

Only fools "declare and decree" that which they have no power to produce as they roll about in fear. Psalm 119 tells us to trust in God's Word. He's got it. If that is the case, then why are we talking so much? *Christ declared and decreed as He marched out of the empty tomb.* Waiting, trusting and knowing allows you to gain your authority to secure God's desires upon the earth. *That* is true courage.

Putting "the cart before the horse" simply makes God look unfaithful because you have forced your desires ahead of God's due to your needs or fear. That is not faith; it is fear and stubbornness. Dare to believe, but believe the Lord, not yourself.

Job did a lot of declaring and decreeing over his children because he was afraid. (See Job 3:25.) He did so before his trials happened. Could it be that this is part and parcel of why the trials came? He had no trust in the beginning, but he was bursting with it in the end.

The only "thing" standing between the answer and its manifestation is the Lord's timing. Pull it away from the enemy in the name of Jesus and then wait on Jesus with a happy heart, as is your pleasure in Christ. Fussing about only makes you a Baal worshiper at Mount Carmel. (See Proverbs 17:22 and 1 Kings 18.)

As we wait for His perfect will and timing in our situations and petitions, there is a stillness to the air as His sweet fragrance invades us. Anxiety kills those moments.

Our portion is to rejoice and be glad, for the answer is on the way. Praise Him on *this side* of the Red Sea while you are waiting; believe me, the waters will part! Psalm 149 says that the "high praises" of the saints "execute" judgment on the enemy, and so it does (verses 6 and 9, KJV).

If Jesus is in charge of one thing, then He is in charge of everything. Lay it down, write it out and let it go. Let Him take it from here. May He find you peacefully and happily waiting as He enters the room where you are. *You cannot wait peacefully if you are afraid, and if you are afraid, you cannot be fearless.* Certainly, no courage is found there.

An insecurity of not knowing if you are taken care of can pound away at the soul and alter identity in a way nobody could ever expect; it causes you to need control and to take it, while directly preventing you from yielding beyond surrender to Him.

To know beyond hoping that the Lord has your good in mind is to trust Him. Don't worry; God has you and everything that concerns you. He will take good care of you. (See Philippians 4:6–7.)

My grandfather, C. O. Hardister, rehearsed this story, along with others, to me many years ago as we would do Bible studies at the kitchen table when I was ten years old. He loved to share stories about how the gospel mattered and how the Holy Spirit was always at work. This was one of my favorites from those days while "at his feet."

Robert Bruce, who was born in the year 1554, was a Revivalist, intercessor and preacher. He would say, later in his life, that all his persecutions just gave him a ladder to climb in order to gain heights toward Christ and that he counted every trial a great privilege. His works led to the Second Great Reformation. He raised up many leaders and like-minded people who would live holy lives to pursue the revival and Reformation. He was told by the religious forces of that day, however, to "calm down, or you will be killed."

Robert Bruce would not calm down. He was a leader within the remnant and was not afraid of the words of those who did not understand his calling or quest. In spite of it all, he changed the world.

As a young man, because he refused to bow to the religious regulations of the king, he took refuge in a cave from a group of people who were seeking his life due to the passion by which he preached the gospel. They spoke very clearly of their intentions to torture and kill him.

A spider, almost at once, wove a web across the mouth of the cave, and when the enemy came by, they saw the web and took for granted that no one had entered that cave for quite some time. [Please know that if Robert Bruce had a fear of spiders, he would have killed that spider upon entering the cave. Fear of any kind is unproductive to the Kingdom of God.]

The destiny of millions of people hinged upon that little spider's web. Sometimes, oftentimes, it appears that God's plan is frustrated, but be patient, for He is working His plan.

Robert Bruce's ability to stand against wickedness and endeavor to please God and not man would be the trademark of his life as the king would banish him. Yet and still he would change the world. It would be said of Robert Bruce at his funeral in 1631, having passed while in his late seventies:

"Wherever he had an opportunity of preaching, great crowds attended; he preached with remarkable power. Because his own life was in full accord with his preaching…the influence attained was almost without parallel in the history of the Scottish Church."

On the day he died, he came to the table and ate an egg. And then he told his daughter:

"I think I am yet hungry, ye may bring me another egg." But instantly he fell into deep prayer and then said, *"Hold, daughter; my Master calls me."* With these words, his sight failed him, and calling for his family Bible, he said, *"Cast up to me the eighth chapter of the epistle to the Romans and set my finger on these words,"* and he recited:

"I am persuaded, that neither death, nor life, nor angels, nor principalities, nor powers, nor things present, nor things to come, nor height, nor depth, nor any other creature, shall be able to separate us from the love of God which is in Christ Jesus our Lord." Then he would say: *"Now, is my finger upon them?"* and being told it was, he said, *"Now, God be with you, my children; I have breakfasted with you, and shall have dinner with my Lord Jesus Christ this night, the King awaits my arrival."*

If Robert Bruce had wanted to please man more than God, his destiny would have been different, and so would the world as we know it. He was fearless because he had enough bravery to find the courage to prevail. The same is true of Paul as he said:

For do I now persuade men, or God? or do I seek to please men? for if I yet pleased men, I should not be the servant of Christ (Galatians 1:10 KJV).

The remnant is full of those who march to a drum that many others cannot hear, a spiritual drum that demands a price be paid and that those who hear it run to the cost, just as Jesus did. (See 1 Corinthians 6:20.) And they are not afraid. The devil is counting on you being a coward; he is banking on your fear. Disappoint him and unravel his plan.

I am a Revivalist, so staying in one place and building an army for the Lord always seemed like a stretch to me...even a ridiculous quest. The Lord told me to do it a couple decades ago, so I did.

And as with most things of obedience, starting The Revival Center has been the greatest blessing and yet the biggest challenge. The blessings far outweigh what I could have imagined. The Lord told me, so long ago, that The Revival Center would not be a regular church but a training center, a ground for saints who are not afraid of a revival lifestyle.

These individuals are willing to pay the price, to deny their flesh and their own desires to get the job done. They do this for the glory of the Lord and for the power of His Kingdom here on this earth. The cry of their heart is "death to self" and "life in Christ." (See Philippians 1:21.)

It has been nothing short of miraculous to watch these people surrender to the Lord. A radical saint is a beautiful sight to observe, as the delight of the Lord is held upon them, rain or shine. Some people cannot do such things that a radical saint does because they get in the way of the process of "death to self" due to their own wants and needs. But the ones who have hung in there and got the job done? Well, you should just see what they will allow the Lord to do through them.

They are the Heralds who shout, the watchmen who warn and the leaders of the army of the remnant; they are soldiers who have chosen this marching song. Maybe you are too...or, I suspect, soon will be.

As you flip through the pages of this book, you will find a spot for yourself, the place perhaps where you quit, or maybe the place you have been looking for in order to complete your quest.

The fear of man is an increasingly alarming and disturbing yet relevant issue. Many Christians are in the grip of this paralyzing mental occupation. It slowly becomes impossible to move in obedience to the Lord's voice if there is a tendency to withdraw out of anxiety or fear of another's opinion or response.

People were infuriated at Jesus and claimed He was a false teacher. He climbed up Calvary's hill anyway. Keep your eye on what the Lord has set before you to do. (See Philippians 3:13–14.) Do it anyway!

There will always be people who love what you do and others who hate what you do. There will always be people who like you and others who dislike you. The key to overcoming this problem is to not give people more power than they possess. If they are allowed to cause you pain, then, in a sense, you are worshiping them and your allegiance is to them. At that point, they have power to destroy your call. Instead, serve the Lord and let the jealous, angry hordes kick rocks.

Jesus is the One who matters. People do matter, yes; they are the job. But they don't matter more than Jesus. He will bring you champions to hold your arms up in the night. He will give you champions who love Him more than anyone else. He will bring you champions who will encourage your heart, especially when you did not know that you needed it.

You may have prayed for the Lord to "move through you," and if this has been your desire, then be certain that the Lord will begin dealing with elements of the fear of man in your life, since He must. *The anointing of God will not rest on fear. It doesn't split lanes or share portions.*

This is a fundamental building block to your Christian life: people cannot matter more than Jesus. I am fairly sure that you are a blessing, but that cannot be the call, the reason or the push.

You cannot maintain your status as a "man pleaser" and "God pleaser" at the same time. You must choose, and if you choose God, the people will get mad—*that* you can count on. Call it "a joy," as James said. (See James 1:2.)

I have heard that we are afraid of what other people think of us because we are too in love with ourselves. That is the truth.

God will take down your tower of self-importance when He deals with your fear of man. You don't have to protect yourself, and you won't if you believe that the Lord is your protector and the captain of your soul.

Our need for affirmation and acceptance from others can, without a doubt, destroy or, at the very least, hinder any impact we would or should have in the Kingdom. It kills our spiritual courage and leaves us for dead on the roadside of effectiveness.

I tell you this: Don't read your fan mail. That is a dangerous occupation. They will love you one day and despise you the next. This cannot matter to you. And it won't, if your identity is in Jesus Christ instead of man.

A need for affirmation and acceptance from others shouts that you do not possess those things from Christ. It means that your identity is not in Him but rather hinges on the thoughts, deeds and intentions of others. The devil can use them anytime he wants to if this is your heart.

I submit to you that if this is the case, then you have, for now, disqualified yourself from *ministry* or leadership and the spiritual battle it requires. Seeking fulfillment from others because you haven't been made well under the hand of God most often leads to a tragic end.

We do not need another gifted person. What we need is a surrendered and yielded person—one whose gifts are tethered to the Cross of Christ and immovable. Without this, we will water down what the Lord has called us to do out of fear of being misunderstood. *Vessels of honor are built, not born.*

To surrender is to let the Lord have His way. To yield is to let the Lord have His way in spite of your desires and concerns; it is a complete trust fall.

Only when we are willing to be misunderstood and unappreciated will we break away from the fear of man. We must not only be willing for it, but also expect it and plan for it.

When you are fighting battles in the spiritual realm, these errors in your soul can create a devastating bondage in you. Fear of man creates the battlefield you will die on. The fear of man will drain the courage to accomplish anything right out of you.

The fear of man will cripple your supernatural giftings and calling while deeming you a vessel of dishonor in the house of God. With all your unresolved issues, you are at risk of becoming a dead body on the battlefield you were called to conquer, forever immortalized as "Willing But Unable." What an incredibly sad and avoidable day that would be.

Whatever opportunity the Lord presents to you, go after it with the zeal of the Lord, holding nothing back. It is in that passion that you will carve out greatness in your life.

Let the bravery you have exhibited by getting this far lend courage to you. Onward!

———————————— ✦ ————————————

"Courage doesn't always roar. Sometimes courage is the quiet voice at the end of the day saying, 'I will try again tomorrow.'"

—Mary Anne Radmacher
From the poem, 1985

———————————— ✦ ————————————

CHAPTER TWO

How Overcomers Overcome

"The only real fatal element in defeat is the resolution to not try again. To try again is to please God. To try again is to expect the Lord to use you for His glory. God does not comfort us to make us comfortable, but to make us comforters. We must at all cost, do what we have to do in order to stand on our feet, especially in the face of adversity."

—John Henry Jowett
The Whole Armour of God, 1916

As we stand tall in the soil of our soul to examine the impasse between where we were and where we are summoned to go, *there is a place between behaving well and being well that we must break free from.* It is the land of compromise that holds prisoners so tightly that they cannot breathe. But there is a place where hypocrisy gives way to honesty and we are able to see our shortcomings. It is *this* place, now, today.

It is okay to not be okay. Once you admit that, you can move on from that place of bondage and begin the journey beyond "okay." Overcomers cannot pretend; they must "know and be" from the fiber of their soul.

Tragedy and disaster have given way to the unique and beautiful things upon the canvas of our lives. It is a tapestry, really, where on one side it doesn't look so bad while it is being worked on, but the other side looks like an absolute train wreck. We try to paint "happy trees," as Bob Ross would instruct, but it all looks like mud and mess from here.

If you choose the side of Christ, then you are obligated to let Him do the work in you and make you ready. As your great journey unfolds and your commitment rises, you find that overcoming your desires and afflictions becomes easier. If you refuse to overcome, then you are refusing to be Christlike and the question stands in front of you, "Do you know Christ at all?"

The Lord allows these hard things to be part of us so that we will have new and original ways to glorify and honor Him in our pain. He does not require it, but our life does. That seems to be the trouble; we pick battles that are ours, not God's, and He is required by His Word to fight the battles that are His, not the ones we choose. (See 1 Samuel 17 and 2 Chronicles 20.)

The collateral damage of our lives seems to keep us in a continuous cycle that prevents us from battling the enemy and, worse yet, our own broken soul.

When our past begins to dictate our future, there is a problem. Decades can go by and our mountaintops collapse into valleys with trodden sod where God is forgotten and what He is able to do is unknown.

It is in those moments that we realize the buried wounds that we clung to were the problem all along, and we have been shadow-boxing, making very slight progress. When something is buried alive; it still has a voice and will move the ground to be heard. It *is* time to be well.

No matter how many times you have failed, remember that this is a new day. Don't bring your fear of failure into today. Decide to go beyond bravery into courage. What was a failure yesterday is only able to duplicate itself today if you allow it.

Be aware that preconception owns perception.

Spirituality runs off a strategic legal system. If it's *not* one hundred percent scriptural, then it's *zero percent* true and effective and should not be considered.

Here are the facts:

- You can do away with the enemy because Christ is in you.
- The devil is counting on you being a coward.
- Keep it simple; then no demon force is out of your league.
- The enemy is the prince of this world, but he has been dethroned; he does not have the keys to his own house. (See 1 Corinthians 2.)

- As you abide in Christ, you will be full of authority.
- Your identity is found in what you surrender to.
- Wounds run to disobedience for safety. Don't let your wounds (or opinions) guide you. You will be tempted to operate in a partial obedience, which is just simply glorified disobedience.

Maybe you just cannot overcome. There is a reason for that. As we approach our understanding of who we are destined to be, it gives way to the journey to sanctification. This is the process of the "overcoming ability."

I would like to outline the process here. But first, let's look at the types of spirits we are dealing with:

Four General Types of Spirits in Spiritual Warfare

1. *Territorial* – This spirit is over a general or regional area.
2. *Controlling* – This spirit rules over spiritual entities.
3. *Oppressive* – This spirit attacks behaviors and thoughts; it comes against your identity. Many people simply think, "This is how I am."
4. *Possessive* – With this type of spirit, your soul is overcome, along with your will, your mind and your spirit. Christians cannot get possessed. When a person is saved, Jesus goes into the spirit. The rest of that person, though, needs to be "saved" as well. *This is the process one undergoes from purification to sanctification.* When an individual finds Christ, the enemy must be told to go, or he will simply abide in other areas of the person and prevent him or her from being an overcomer while demonizing and oppressing the person's soul. (See 1 John 5:4–5 and Revelation 21:7.)

This is why there are so many Christians who cannot overcome. They cannot move beyond the terror of the past, the disappointment of their life, or the fear of the future. They are stuck trying to purify, never accomplishing it and never moving on. They are stuck in a maddening cycle of flesh and desire. The anointing of Jesus Christ cannot live in such a state. We are not called to be perfect, but we are called to be overcomers. (See Romans 8:37.)

As our spirit becomes bigger, the spiritual increases and spills over into other areas of our life. (Likewise, as our flesh grows, the flesh spills over into other areas of our life as well, while minimizing our spirit.)

In the following visual, you can see, as you put a small J (for Jesus) in a box with your name, that you are almost equal. As you fill your spirit up with the things of God and are fervent toward them, the Jesus in your spirit gets bigger. Eventually He becomes bigger than you. Then finally He spills over into your soul, and the process completes itself in your body and your mind. When all four sections are full of the "Big J" for Jesus, you are sanctified. It's more of Him, less of you.

Taking the ailments of your body, soul and mind with you, which we discussed earlier, won't work. You will never make the climb. The baggage will turn into luggage, and it will be too heavy. Use the tools you have learned so far, practice them and walk them out. Then you will dance across the following pages.

Our spiritual walk: Purification ➔ Consecration ➔ Sanctification

The Jesus Cube

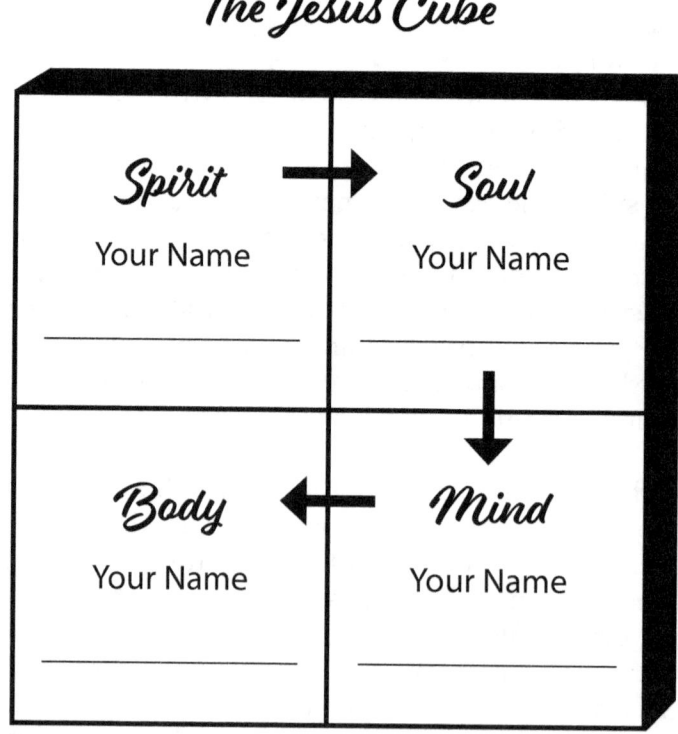

Hebrews 12:1 Therefore, since we are surrounded by so great a cloud of witnesses, let us also lay aside every weight, and sin which clings so closely, and let us run with endurance the race that is set before us.

2 Corinthians 5:17 Therefore, if anyone is in Christ, he is a new creation. The old has passed away; behold, the new has come.

Spirit

Hebrews 9:14 How much more will the blood of Christ, who through the eternal Spirit offered himself without blemish to God, purify our conscience from dead works to serve the living God.

1 Thessalonians 5:23 Now may the God of peace himself sanctify you completely, and may your whole spirit and soul and body be kept blameless at the coming of our Lord Jesus Christ.

1 Corinthians 3:16 Do you not know that you are God's temple and that God's Spirit dwells in you?

1 John 1:9 If we confess our sins, he is faithful and just to forgive us our sins and to cleanse us from all unrighteousness.

Soul

Colossians 3:2 Set your minds on things that are above, not on things that are on earth.

John 17:17 Sanctify them in the truth; your word is truth.

1 John 3:3 And everyone who thus hopes in him purifies himself as he is pure.

1 Peter 1:22 Having purified your souls by your obedience to the truth for a sincere brotherly love, love one another earnestly from a pure heart.

Body

2 Corinthians 4:16 So we do not lose heart. Though our outer self is wasting away, our inner self is being renewed day by day.

2 Corinthians 7:1 Since we have these promises, beloved, let us cleanse ourselves from every defilement of body and spirit, bringing holiness to completion in the fear of God.

Romans 7:18—25

Romans 12:1 I appeal to you therefore, brothers, by the mercies of God, to present your bodies as a living sacrifice, holy and acceptable to God, which is your spiritual worship.

Mind

1 Peter 1:13 Therefore, preparing your minds for action, and being sober-minded, set your hope fully on the grace that will be brought to you at the revelation of Jesus Christ.

Romans 12:2 Do not be conformed to this world, but be transformed by the renewal of your mind, that by testing you may discern what is the will of God, what is good and acceptable and perfect.
Philippians 4:8 Finally, brothers, whatever is true, whatever is honorable, whatever is just, whatever is pure, whatever is lovely, whatever is commendable, if there is any excellence, if there is anything worthy of praise, think about these things.
Ephesians 4:23 And be renewed in the spirit of your minds.

Purification – This is where you make decisions to be Christ-like. You believe and accept Jesus as Lord of your life, you read the Word and you do what is right and pleasing to the Lord. Your habits change. Your desires change. One step at a time, you give Him control. *Here you hope.*

Consecration – This is where you commit to those decisions. You seek to walk in right choices and forsake the situations and things that will pull you back into your "old life." Your relationships change. Here is where you must commit. *Here you believe.*

Sanctification –This is where you walk in those decisions. It is the place you arrive at when you have gone through purification and consecration. Sanctification is where you live, where the things that bothered you before don't bother you anymore because you are sanctified.

When you are sanctified, you find it easier to fight hell because you are not fighting yourself or those around you. You don't complain about the wilderness and the valleys because those were the things you went through to get sanctified. You recognize their great value. You stop finding fault and fighting people to justify yourself.

Opportunities and challenges present themselves during the purification and consecration processes because you need them to move you on to sanctification. Once you are sanctified, you go through trials in a godlier manner; you swiftly seek to glorify and honor God. Satan has a hard time tripping you up in the place of sanctification. Vessels of honor are built here. *Here you know.*

I suppose the ultimate desire in all of this is for us to be a vessel fit for the Master's use. Working with the precious Holy Spirit to accomplish the desires of the Lord is the most beautiful thing of all. When we have strongholds from wounds rooted in our soul, we are not effectively trustworthy in ministry of any kind.

Even if you are not interested in ministry or have a desire to bless others, being tangled up with your past just clearly causes you to be, shall we say, "not the best version of yourself." It is tough being a human when you cannot or, that is, refuse to commit.

Our gifts are made to move through our callings. We must always yield to God in our calling, not yield to our gifting. When we allow our gift to lead us, then we are not anchored in the Cross but in our own desires or even in the needs that someone else presents to us. Someone else's need cannot bear upon us more greatly than what God has told us to do...or not do.

God loves our heart most of all. The greatest calling is to love Jesus. However, here I am trying to show you that He is asking us to be His hands and feet to reach a broken world. He is asking us to allow Him to use us. We are often so busy ministering to our own pain that we can't hear Him. It is time to be well and minister to others.

I don't doubt that you may be an emotional cripple, and I don't doubt that it is terrible, but I do doubt that you are supposed to stay that way.

Consider the following tests and checklist of bondages as we walk through this journey together. This is your prescribed course. You will be made well. The depths of Christ and His great anointing are hovering, waiting for one in whom God can show Himself strong. (See 2 Chronicles 16:9.) This is you, for you hold in your hands a rule book on how to get there.

As you are going from purification to consecration to sanctification, dealing with the wounds that ail your soul, you must go through the mandate of Abraham. This is a road worth walking, and it takes a lifetime to perfect it. So, you see, there is no time to stop marching and find a chair to watch the parade as it goes by.

I offer you these questions within "The 12 Applications of Abraham (Abram)" so that you can measure yourself and stay hidden within the Lord. All of us must walk these tests out in one way or another, at various stages of our lives, even over and over, and often many of them at the same time.

The 12 Applications of Abraham (Abram)

1. **Obedience** – Genesis 12:1–7
    Test – Abram left Ur and Haran for an unknown destination in obedience to God.
    Application – Do I trust God for my future? Is His will part of my decision-making process?

2. **Peace** – Genesis 13:8–13
    Test – Abraham directed a peaceful separation from Lot.
    Application – Do I trust God with my interests even when it appears that I am being treated unfairly?

3. **Faithfulness** – Genesis 14:13–18
    Test – Abraham rescued Lot from the five kings.
    Application – Does my faithfulness to others bear witness to my trust in God?

4. **Tithing** – Genesis 14:17–24
    Test – Abraham gladly gave a tithe to the king of Salem but refused the gift of the king of Sodom.
    Application – Am I careful to give God honor when I am dealing with others? God wanted Abraham to be a giver, so the tithe, which he willingly gave, strategically came before he was asked to offer up his son.

    He refused to allow a heathen king to partake in the Glory of God over him. He may have needed financial help, but he would rather wait on God to fulfill His promises to him than receive from that which was evil.

5. **Surrender** – Genesis 15:1–6
    Test – Abraham had to trust God that he would have a son.
    Application – How often do I consciously reaffirm my trust in God's promises?

6. **Believe** – Genesis 15:7–11
    Test – Abraham received the promised land by faith, and that promise would not be fulfilled for many generations.
    Application – How have I demonstrated my trust in God?

7. **Submission** – Genesis 17:9–27
    Test – Abraham, at God's command, circumcised every man in his family.
    Application – At what occasions in my life did I act in disobedience or in obedience? (By these, you will understand your strengths and weaknesses.)

8. **Hospitality** – Genesis 18:1–8
   Test – Abraham welcomed strangers.
   Application – When was the last time I genuinely practiced hospitality?

9. **Prayer** – Genesis 18:22–33
   Test – Abraham prayed for Sodom.
   Application – Do I want them saved, or do I want them punished?

10. **Confession** – Genesis 20:1–17
    Test – Abraham admitted to wrongdoing, repented and made it right.
    Application – Do I cover up my sin, or do I confess it? (If you hurt somebody, you need to say you are sorry and make it right. Seek forgiveness according to Matthew 5)

11. **Honesty** – Genesis 21:22–34
    Test – Abraham negotiated a treaty with Abimelech for a well.
    Application – Can people depend on my word or count on my promises?

12. **Trust** – Genesis 22:12
    Test – Abraham prepared to sacrifice his son—laying it all down, even a promise. A person can't love a promise more than they love the Lord.
    Application – In what ways has my life demonstrated that I will not allow anything to go in front of God?

Often, when we have been made well, our body, soul and mind fight the process and prefer to live in the cheap real estate where we resided before. The low rent district doesn't ask for much. I offer these "10 Characteristics of Bondage" for you to measure yourself by in order to stay hidden in the Lord.

You will also want to check yourself as time goes by. These things happen slowly and have the power to bring an onslaught of disaster if they are not dealt with.

10 Characteristics of Bondage

1. **Orphan attitude** – You feel sad, believe you have no support and are constantly lonely.
2. **Victim's heart** – You always think that you need to act out, thus sabotaging your success.

3. **Guilty soul** – You feel that you've done something wrong. Do not carry guilt. Repent and be done with it, or it will work itself into shame.

4. **Shame** – This is how you feel about what you did. All things are new in Christ, and *that* should be your truth.

5. **Condemnation** – The accusing voice of the enemy wars against who you are in Christ. This is not the conviction of the Holy Spirit.

6. **Pride** – Beyond the obvious, pride often disguises itself as false humility and glorified disobedience. (God says to go right and I go left because I don't want to go right, and I try to pass off the decision as godly, since I am at least moving in a direction.)

7. **Insecurity** – Insecurity disguises itself as intellect, and it is brought on by unresolved wounds and by comparing oneself to others and not to Christ. It can also disguise itself as overt prideful security, which is brought on by rejection and unworthiness stemming from past unresolved wounds. The need to be right and the assumption that others are always attacking you will be prevalent. It is narcissistic at its root.

8. **Doubt** – Doubt disguises itself as curiosity. Doubt produces a mistrust and comes from feeling unworthy. It becomes a root in your life and forms the strongholds of unbelief, anger and bitterness.

9. **Judgment** – Judgment rises up and replaces Godly discernment.

10. **Faith with no trust** – Trust is mature faith and cannot develop with bondages and unresolved wounds.

Fear brings pride because humility brings vulnerability. To be vulnerable, you cannot be afraid. Perfect love is knowing you are loved and worthy in Christ. (See 1 John 5:11–13.)

As we decrease bad behavior and increase praise, we find that we are beginning to believe what we pray.

You will get there because Romans 8:32 says that since God didn't spare His only Son, why would He withhold anything from us? It just takes time and trust. We must be willing to fight for our promises and, at the same time, get out of the way. The Lord Jesus is big enough to handle even us. Let Him.

All our wounds from the past, all the fears, disappointments and doubts, belong in a box—a casket, a coffin—along with our false identities before Christ. We are redeemed and worthy. Anything else is worshiping the "wrong Jesus," surely not the One marching out of an empty tomb in power.

Your old self needs to be buried. Killed and buried. Buried deep. If that old self tries to resurrect itself, remind it that it is in a coffin, there was a funeral, it is dead and there is no hope of life for it. That ground cannot rattle and shake you off balance. Walk away. The grave doesn't need you to visit it with flowers! (See Romans 6:6–23.)

Darrell Robinson wrote in *People Sharing Jesus*:

> From Texas history comes the story of the conversion of Sam Houston, who passed away in 1863. At one time, the Texas hero was called "The Old Drunk." While he was governor of Tennessee, his wife left him. In despair he resigned as governor and tried to escape his problems by going to live among Cherokee Indians.
>
> He stayed drunk much of the time. It is said that the Indians, as they walked through the forest, would have to move him out of the path where he lay in a stupor.
>
> He married the daughter of a preacher and later converted to Christianity, but he still had some of his old tendencies. One day as he rode along a trail, his horse stumbled. Houston spontaneously cursed, reverting to his old habit.
>
> Immediately he was convicted of his sin. He got off his horse, knelt down on the trail, and cried out to God for forgiveness. Houston had already received Christ, but God was teaching him to live in fellowship with him moment by moment. As soon as the Holy Spirit made Sam Houston aware of his sin, he confessed it and stopped doing it (p. 17).

Sam Houston was a man who had decided he would be an overcomer and was not going to let anything get in the way, no matter how small.

Compare your choices, reactions and decisions against these pages and decide to be made well. Decide to do the work and then jump into what the Lord has gifted and called you to do. This is your time to finally be well. The Holy Spirit has great power to deliver; it is one of His favorite things to do.

May your identity shine as "spotless" in Christ Jesus, having paid the price that was required of you as you march up the hill to take down what holds you back. As you confidently walk in your God-given overcoming ability, you will find yourself being courageous and fearless, holding every blessing.

Later, he went to Texas, where he became the great hero of the Texas revolution when he routed General Santa Ana's Mexican army. Houston's battle cry, "Remember the Alamo!" helped win independence for Texas.

——————————— ✦ ———————————

"Your hardest times often lead to the greatest moments of your life. Keep going. Tough situations build strong people in the end."

—Roy T. Bennett
The Light in the Heart, 2016

——————————— ✦ ———————————

CHAPTER THREE

Unshackled in Liberty – Determined in the Desert

"There is no success without sacrifice. If you succeed without sacrifice, it is because someone has suffered before you. If you sacrifice without success, it is because someone will succeed after you. All for His glory — I have obeyed my Lord."

—Adoniram Judson,
upon the death of his wife while he was imprisoned[1]
Adoniram Judson: A Biography, 1883

There is a holy arrangement that must be managed in our soul in order for us to walk as the Lord intends. This arrangement extends beyond our salvation to what our salvation holds for the Kingdom of God. We receive salvation as a gift, pretty bow and all. But do we open the package to see what is inside? Or do we just carry the present around, declaring that we have this gift?

Our life must be spotless, as the Word says in Jude 23 (KJV): we are to hate "even the garment spotted by the flesh." It is a pursuit of uncommon Christianity, the endeavor to get "Egypt" out of our heart.

---

1 The full story of Adoniram Judson here is inspiring. He was in a Burmese prison when his young wife, Ann Judson, succumbed to smallpox in 1826 while caring for their infant son. His words about success and sacrifice, which are quoted above, are what he said upon hearing of her death. He followed what he believed; Adoniram Judson went on to serve in Burma (India) for forty years and outlived two more wives. Only six of his eleven children survived, and yet, because his heart was set on the goal before him, he never quit. He started sixty-three churches and was responsible for tens of thousands of souls coming to the Kingdom of God.

Spotless is not perfect. Spotless is doable. Spotless means that you love Jesus more than the world, and your life shows it.

To do that, to live like that, is no accident; it is a purposeful push toward a call bigger than we can hold. We make enough mistakes on accident; to start making them on purpose is plain stupid.

Perfection, in our way of understanding, is quite ridiculous, but in God's understanding, it is a heartfelt move toward Him and attainable. As we walk with Him, we are perfect in heart first, then the rest follows. He told Abraham (Abram), "Walk before me, and be thou perfect" (Genesis 17:1 KJV; the English Standard Version says "blameless").

Without the help of the Holy Spirit, it surely *is* an impossible task. We are not perfect (blameless), and God knows that, but the mandate is there, so we lean upon the Holy Spirit to work it out in us.

A wilderness time, a time in a deserted place, is often needed. We cannot believe for all the promises the Lord intends to give to us unless we have taken a very long tour in the wilderness. Time in the wilderness tunes our ears and fixes every part of who we were while measuring who we are against who God intends for us to be.

The wilderness heals wounds, destroys a selfish heart and ushers us into a place where there is no cost too high for the Kingdom of God to be enlarged here on this earth for the glory of God.

God is endeavoring to raise up a remnant within His army, and beyond them, leaders, or generals, heralds who will train and lead that remnant to destroy the darkness of the enemy and accomplish God's design and desire.

I see that the world has brought forward its heartbeat into Christianity. People seem to want a "ministry" and a "calling" beyond a life that pays a price with fasting, praying and giving what one doesn't have, in the wilderness, to hear the Lord clearly. *People seem to be satisfied with a relationship because fellowship would take too much time and require too much effort.*

The wilderness is a place of visitation. "Prepare ye in the wilderness...make straight in the desert," cries the prophet. (See Isaiah 40:3–5 and Mark 1:3.) We should not be surprised to discover that God does not often choose the well-watered garden, the fruitful field or the lush forest as the scene of a divine visitation, for they have no need.

He chooses, rather, the dry and weary land, parched and barren, whose yawning cracks plead to heaven for showers; it is here that God is pleased to appear within the storms of the Spirit. God therefore chooses the place that provides the greatest scope for the demonstration of His glory. This cost produces a liberty, a determination and a courage that we can receive no other way.

When something amazing happens, people shout, "This is the finger of God!" They acknowledge that "the exceeding greatness of the power" that has accomplished the miracle must be of God and not of men, and so the Lord alone is exalted in that day. (See Ephesians 1:19–23.)

But then that day passes, and people must realize who they are and what they are unwilling to do for Jesus. At that point, everything looks different, and the truth emerges. Can you hear Jesus well enough to raise the dead or not? Can you hear Jesus well enough to cast demons out or not? Can you hear Jesus well enough to actively forgive, the most horrific crime against you? Can you hear Jesus well enough to bring your spirit higher than your flesh, or are you okay watching others get the job done as you sit on your lawn chair? *The iced tea will run out eventually, and the weather will change. In fact, it is changing now.*

So, what is your portion? I will tell you what it is. For now, it is a wilderness. Pace it out in steps, live there, walk it until you memorize it, run it until you sweat blood, and then—and only then—will it rise up and become a garden. Not before, for there are no shortcuts.

Life is portioned out to us not only in moments and seasons, but also in times. Three specific events happened at the Cross of Christ. And they happened at three different, specific times: 9:00 in the morning, noon and 3:00 in the afternoon. Ask the Lord what time it is. Being in the wilderness is not enough; you have to know what to do there. You may be in the wilderness, but have you stepped out of your "time zone"?

You may be doing the right thing at exactly the wrong time. Perhaps you are protecting that "wound" and almost hold it as precious. Nothing is sacred in the wilderness, except for Christ. Let it all go and find redemption.

A wilderness place is where you deny yourself absolutely everything and seek the Lord for a pure heart; it must not have anything of you. God will visit you there as you endeavor to destroy the last stronghold...*which is you.* Which is me. All of our wounds and terrors cannot breathe in the desert place where we are fasting and praying and endeavoring to hear our Lord like never before.

23

"Wilderness" is that land that the farmer looks upon as unworkable and therefore hopeless. Maybe that word is a fitting description of the sphere of your spiritual activities, of that which has been for so long the scene of your travail and tears, your labors and longings.

With fasting and praying, we go to the wilderness. There we find the Lord as we have never seen Him before: *with joy unspeakable and full of glory as we go from our glory to His.*

When it seems like a sheer impossibility that there should be a work of God in you, take heed to the command in Isaiah 40:3 (KJV): "Prepare ye the way of the LORD [in the wilderness], make straight in the desert a highway," for God has promised that "the wilderness and the solitary place shall be glad for them; and the desert shall rejoice, and blossom as the rose" (Isaiah 35:1 KJV).

Isaiah 35 reminds us that the God to whom no situation is impossible, has chosen the wilderness as the place in which to manifest His power and glory.

As I have said before, *without pain, there is no power.*

Isaiah 35:3–7 (KJV) declares, as no man can: "Strengthen ye the weak hands, and confirm the feeble knees. Say to them that are of a fearful heart, Be strong, fear not: behold, your God will come with vengeance, even God with a recompence; he will come and save you....for in the wilderness shall waters break out, and streams in the desert...."

Maybe you have been in the wilderness for a while. Maybe it is unrelenting, and your windblown, sand-torn body bears its marks. All I can say is that I was there and that the wilderness has a cause. There is a reason beyond your knowing. Your spiritual wilderness soon enough will be transformed into a paradise.

Draw close to the fruit of the Spirit in Christ and take inventory there. In the following pages, you will find tools to identify the possible problems that have held you back.

It may be a trial of your own doing, such as disobedience, an injustice handed to you as a gift; or perhaps it is simply the Holy Spirit's chiseling you like a beautiful piece of marble to present to the Lord. Whatever the case may be, don't leave the desert and choose cheap living because the process is too hard.

The truth is that it will get easier once you make the first strike, so just hold on. You will fight your way out with the weapons of the Spirit and your will to do so. Get through this book, get through the tests and trials of your wilderness, and see if God Himself doesn't reveal a clear path out for you. Before this wonderful work of transformation can take place, a way must be prepared, a highway must be made straight.

How is it to be done? "Beginning with me" is the first step. Verse 8 of Isaiah 35 (KJV) says, "And an highway shall be there, and a way, and it shall be called The way of holiness...." The Lord has probably been telling you to offer something up to Him. Maybe your fear is preventing your hands from lifting it up to Him, but the day for that fear is over.

We each need to pause and ask ourselves, "Is my heart, my life, a highway of holiness for God? Have I swept away the stones of unbelief and dashed hopes? Have the crooked places of unrighteousness been made straight? Have I taken up the stumbling blocks of inconsistency, doubt and worldliness? When the God of holiness moves in the irresistible power of who He is, will He call me 'ready'?"

If you cannot answer "yes" to these questions, lay down your heart and seek the Lord. Perhaps you try sometimes and it is too difficult. *I tell you it is difficult because you are not sold out to the idea.* It must be a selfless quest, one that of a surety blesses Jesus, and for us...well, we aren't the point.

J. Hudson Taylor, who spent fifty-one years as a missionary to China, in 1885 said, "It is not so much the greatness of our troubles, as the littleness of our spirit, which makes us complain."

This complaining bears down upon our belief system. Don't allow it. Crush it. March out in obedience as the others shout, "It will never work." The longer you stay around that behavior, the quicker it becomes part of you, and when that happens, the joy of the journey is gone.

I have heard people say, "It is not about the journey, but the destination." Wrong! It is completely all about the journey and what you are allowing God to create in you so that you can dwell in the destination with a powerful, abiding force unto God alone.

This is why Jesus told Peter, when he was speaking puffed-up words to the Savior, "Get behind me, Satan" (Matthew 16:23 NIV). Jesus wasn't going to hear the bad report because He couldn't afford to be distracted. People are not going to like it when you follow God completely, but that is okay; you are not serving them, and your goal is not to glorify them but Christ.

James 1:8 (KJV) says, "A double minded man is unstable in all his ways." To be onboard with everything God is about to do, to crave it and desire it above yourself, you have to care more about His Kingdom than your own. Love for the causes of Christ with a passion to defend them will be birthed from the wilderness.

If you are not single-minded in God's design, then you will be left on the sidelines, anchored in doubt, dealing with your dreadful self, as the warriors march through your field to secure the victory in battle for your liberty. And make no mistake, liberty and freedom are very different.

Freedom is the power or right to act. Liberty is the exercise of that power or right. They are as different as bravery and courage. As we have found, bravery will dream to do a thing—but courage will do it.

David Brainerd lived a short twenty-nine years, passing away in 1747. He was a student at Yale and was expelled for challenging the faculty's right to stop the move of God among the students. Many great people have cited him as their inspiration. He was an evangelist and missionary to the Delaware Indian tribes and died of tuberculosis. He was careful to do the most with what time he had here on this earth. Are we?

In his biography in the *Biographical Dictionary of Christian Missions*, it is stated:

> God could flow unhindered through him. The omnipotence of grace was neither arrested nor straitened by the conditions of his heart; the whole channel was broadened and cleaned out for God's fullest and most powerful passage, so that God with all His mighty forces could come down on the hopeless, savage wilderness and transform it into His blooming, fruitful garden.
>
> He said in the year of his death, "All my desire is in the conversion of the heathen and all my hope is in God: God does not suffer me to be pleased or comforted with hopes of seeing friends or returning to my dear acquaintances to enjoy worldly comforts. Thru my cough and pain, I shall praise and pursue Him."

Here was one who truly prepared the way of the Lord in his own life, so God saw to it that His glory was revealed through him. A sanctified man! God accomplished miraculous things at the hands of Brother Brainerd. How great is the heavenly reward for one who ran to the cost. What is God accomplishing at your hands?

When it comes to the mighty movements of the Spirit, every heart is either a highway or a hindrance.

The spread of the gospel of Jesus and a revival of purity and power sweeping the land truly begins in us, but it does not end there. There must be a sense of responsibility toward our fellow believers who do not yet feel the need or see the possibilities of the hour. Habakkuk 2:2 (KJV) says, "Write the vision, and make it plain...that he may run that readeth it."

Until the vision is written, others will never read; until others read, they will never run as people with a mission, sent by the Spirit of God. The vision must be written upon our heart, upon our lips and upon our life if the way of the Lord is to be prepared in the lives of others.

There must be expectancy in our praying, passion in our preaching, boldness in our planning and holiness in our living if we are to stir those around us and be effective for the Kingdom of God.

Isaiah 40:5 (KJV) is a promise that expresses the very nature and purpose of God's design: "And the glory of the LORD shall be revealed, and all flesh shall see it together...."

According to Psalm 50:3 (KJV), when we have prepared the way of the Lord in our heart and in the hearts of others, then "our God shall come, and shall not keep silence: a fire shall devour before him...."

We must expect a spiritual revolution if our wilderness is to be transformed into the garden of the Lord. *God will see to the revolution if we will provide Him with the space to move.*

Give God a highway, and He promises in Isaiah 40:4–5 (KJV) that "every valley shall be exalted, and every mountain and hill shall be made low: and the crooked shall be made straight, and the rough places plain: and the glory of the LORD shall be revealed, and all flesh shall see it together: for the mouth of the LORD hath spoken it."

This is the revolution of a personal reformation: the wilderness turned upside down and inside out. God is promising that this visitation will bring a reversal of values and a transformation of conditions—in your family, your community, your state and your nation. But first, in your heart.

Mountains of pride, unbelief, materialism, worldly cares, pleasures, ambitions and lusts will flow down and melt at the presence of the Lord, having been made powerless. This is what God promises to do in the visitations of our personal reformations. As we lay low, we lift up Jesus.

Do you want your family to change, salvations around you, your country to change? Count the cost and know that it will take a shift, first in your own life, to accomplish God's desires. The sacrifice is always worth it. (See Luke 14:28.)

In 1838, just five weeks after their wedding, James Calvert and his wife, Mary, went out as missionaries to the cannibals of the Fiji Islands. The ship's captain would say that he himself was not a religious man, maybe not even a good man, but he, in good conscience, could not leave them there. He said he would come back in three days' time.

The captain said, "They are savages and hate Christians for they challenge the authority of the Chiefs, you cannot stay here, you will both die." The couple refused to listen, and instead, with arms outstretched and his voice raised, James Calvert said, "We died before we came." (See Ministry127.com.)

They stayed eighteen years and saved Fiji for Christ. What radical obedience. What a price. What a glory.

Here is the highest and holiest part of being restored to Christ in the fullest extent of His heart: *the manifestation of God, the shining forth of His glory before the eyes of mankind. It is a saint willing to change, the soul who, like Isaiah, has caught a glimpse of that effulgent glory—and one glimpse is enough to spoil us for all our remaining days on earth.*

"Who will go forth?" is the question that God was asking in Isaiah 6 and throughout the Word of God. He is still asking today, "Who will go forth?" Who will live like he or she means it, whatever the cost, to obey the divine command by preparing the way of the Lord, that mankind may behold the glory of God and be changed—forever changed? And with that, has become willing to lose his or her life for Christ in faithfulness to His heart and His house, ever willing to fulfill the call of the remnant?

God intends to honor the remnant with a revival that will visit itself upon mankind for generations to come. But first, we must engage in our personal reformation, a revival lifestyle, one that yields to Christ and loves others, fully equipped in the fruit of the Spirit, far beyond the gifts of the Spirit.

This doesn't happen because you want to be comfortable. It happens because you are loved and want to love others as extravagantly as it has been modeled to you by a powerful and loving God.

God doesn't just love you; He loves you at the cost of His Son.

Before Isaiah said in chapter 6, "Send me," he said, "Woe is me," and he said it because he was "a man of unclean lips" (Isaiah 6:5 KJV). A hot coal to the lips is no joke. It is only the one who refuses to believe or understand what he or she is being prepared for, who will shrink back from it; all the rest run to it.

May we run to the coal and spit at the cost.

Zaccheus had to climb a tree. Abraham had to leave his land and his people. Blind Bartimaeus had to throw off his coat, and the Shunammite had to be willing to cross the threshold into receiving a promise. At some point, we all will be required to lay some things down, if not everything.

> *But we all, with open face beholding as in a glass the glory of the Lord, are changed into the same image from glory to glory, even as by the Spirit of the Lord* (2 Corinthians 3:18 KJV).

Believers spend far too much time praying, "God, change my circumstances...change my coworkers...change my family situation... change the conditions in my life." Yet we seldom pray the most important prayer: "Change me, Lord. I am the one who stands in need of prayer." (See Psalm 51:10.)

God orchestrates the steps and lives of all His children who obey Him and walk in His commands. He does not allow anything to happen to you merely by happenstance or fate. And believe it or not, He has allowed your crisis. What is He trying to tell you through it? (See Psalm 37, Isaiah 26, Proverbs 3 and Romans 8.)

Like it or not, we are all in the process of changing in one way or another. In the spiritual realm, there is no such thing as mere existence; we are continually being changed, either for good or for bad. We are either becoming more like our Lord or more like the world (being influenced by Satan), either growing in Christ or backsliding.

Are you becoming more like Jesus? Are you looking soberly in the mirror each day and praying, "Lord, I want to conform to Your image in every area of my life," as Romans 8:28 says? Or has bitterness taken root, turning into rebellion and hardness of heart? (See Psalm 51:10, Romans 12:2, Mark 6:52 and Matthew 28:17.)

Let me plainly say that if you shield yourself from the convicting Word of God and the voice of His Spirit, then your life will become more chaotic and your situation will worsen. I urge you to cry out to the Lord honestly in prayer: "Help me, change me, O God. Dig deep within me and show me where I have failed and gone wrong." Being willing to see our own errors is tantamount to being reconciled to God's heart.

We are to be Spirit-filled, Spirit-led disciples of Jesus Christ, pushing the boundaries back of religion so that the Cross can be plainly seen.

We are being called to bring our wounds to the Cross of Calvary so we can hear the proclamation of the Lord in the wilderness and receive His promises as we shout with the Moravians, "May the Lamb that was slain receive the reward for His suffering." This is the eternal quest: His happiness, not ours; His desires, not ours. Ours will come in time, but ours cannot be the focus.

Most of the encroachments in the Church came about because apathy had seized the believers. People began to seek their own good above God's. My son Donny used to say, "The righteous should hold integrity to their throat like a knife."

We often give our weapons over to the enemy because they are too heavy to hold. And in that moment, the enemy takes ground—ground that is difficult to regain unless we are serious about taking it back.

Every instance of your life has taught you something. Perhaps you counted it as a joy immediately or maybe it seemed like a wretched curse that you would never overcome and barely endure. But ultimately, in the end, you can find good and move on. You can do that even now as you sit and ponder here on this page. The Lord has great confidence in you, and I believe all of heaven is cheering for you to accomplish what is set before you. THIS you can do!

Walking on water is not hard; getting out of the boat is!

———————— ✦ ————————

"As long as anything in this world means anything to you, your freedom is only a word. You are like a bird that is held by a leash; you can only fly so far."
—François Fénelon
Letter XXX, *Spiritual Letters*, early 1700s

———————— ✦ ————————

CHAPTER FOUR

Which Jesus?

"I know enough to know that I never want to walk without God's peace, joy and His guidance. Testing that knowledge comes at a price I'll forever be unwilling to pay. Could I walk away? Could I live without Him? Yes. But I can't un-know the peace and rest that comes from recognizing His guidance and submitting to His plans for me."
—Cynthia Querin Reynoso
Personal letter, 2025

The question that we must ask ourselves when reaching for a deeper fellowship with Christ that goes beyond a mere relationship is this: "Which Jesus do I serve?" There are four to choose from. The first Jesus is *in a manger*.

We tell this Jesus when to eat and what to eat. We tell Him what to wear and what to say and when to say it. We keep Him wrapped up to bring us comfort, and when He starts to agitate us, we can easily have someone else "hold Him."

When we encounter a baby in a manger, it is easy to keep walking and ignore the cries if we want to. If we haven't counted the cost before we came to Him, we can become resentful of Him because He interrupts our life too much.

The main reason finding a deeper fellowship with Christ is difficult for some is that they did not choose to die to themselves when they chose to follow Him. They want Jesus to stay as a baby in a manger

31

so that they can remain in charge, having decided not to yield to Him. They are holding baby Jesus, but probably not for very long.

The second Jesus is *hanging on the Cross.*

We see Him there and are sad. We weep over Him, and we weep over ourselves. The Cross is everything, don't get me wrong; *never* discount it or take it for granted. We should know what happened there to our dear Friend and Savior. We should know the why of it and be grateful and forever changed.

However, having a deeper fellowship with Christ is difficult when we are consumed with sitting in His blood, at the foot of the Cross, ruminating and weeping over our grief and shame. Our fellowship with Him stalls because we never apply its meaning to our life.

As long as we keep Jesus on the Cross of Calvary, we will never be required to accomplish anything. We will never be compelled to walk out the Scripture to be a living stone, salt or a witness; we will fail at the Great Commission. When we are sitting in the blood, refusing to apply it, we waste it and refuse the authority of it.

Not one soul around you will be delivered of demons or of him or herself because you are too consumed with crying about yourself and everything around you. There will be few salvations, if any. There is power in that blood—power to save and deliver. Power to overcome and heal. There is a trauma movement out there in the world that insists you need to be heard, over and over. You don't! Snap out of it and get over to the tomb.

As we sit there crying at the foot of the Cross, it appears that we love Jesus—as long as we don't have to obey Him or accomplish His will. But, really, *is that love?* After all, in Scripture, Jesus says that if you love Him, you will obey Him. (See John 14:15–31.)

When we say that we are too sad or too addicted or too broken, then our tears become a weapon that we use against the causes of Christ. In all our sorrow, we can actually commit crimes against the Cross. Grief is real—I am not telling you to not feel your grief. I am telling you to not be grief-stricken by allowing grief to rule your life.

Keith Carroll, in "Who Did Calvary Really Seek to Reconcile?" says this:

> Calvary was God's effort to reveal His forgiving nature to us. It was His way of declaring to all mankind that His forgiveness covers the whole world, everyone. The Cross did not reconcile God to man but was God's effort to restore our intimate fellowship with His presence.

The third Jesus is *lying in a tomb.*

He is sealed up. And, as we lie there waiting. hoping, wishing, hardly believing, we are tempted to only observe from afar and not respond as Jesus stands up and His graveclothes fall away to reveal His majesty that most surely will demand a response.

The tomb is not a vacation spot. It is not a condominium. It is the place where you get real with who Christ is and what is holding you back from being just like Him.

Graveclothes represent our wounds and unforgiveness; they are the very foundation of our disbelief and hypocrisy. Somehow, we come up with the idea that the gravestone will be too hard to move, forever discounting that it will always be God's job to do the heavy lifting. That ability to trust seals faith upon us and within us. If we stay in the tomb too long, we start calling it home and monograming the towels. You were not made to live there; it is barely a visiting place.

The Bible says in John 3 that God gave Jesus faith *without* measure. Jesus is in us, so where is His kind of faith? I believe we have buried it alive with all our other living, breathing, agitated wounds that have not been dealt with. Now and again, we can hear it moaning to be dug up and released—but that looks like work.

When we worship an unresurrected Jesus, we will never respond to the plea of the Holy Spirit to fully glorify Jesus, and thereby we can never experience a deeper fellowship with Jesus through the Holy Spirit.

The fourth Jesus is *walking out of the tomb.*

This Jesus walks out with resurrection power and demands a response. We cannot walk in His authority if we do not have our identity in Him. (Just read about the seven sons of Sceva, the chief of the priests, and the demoniac in Acts 19:11–20.) We cannot walk in His authority if we have no dominion, and we can only get dominion through identity in Him.

We cannot walk in His authority if we are easily or often offended. We cannot walk in His authority if we harbor unforgiveness or grief like a privilege. We cannot walk in His authority if we refuse to operate in the fruit of the Spirit. We cannot walk in Christ's authority if we are busy doing the things that He hates. (See Proverbs 6:16–19.)

When we walk outside of the Lord's protection, we will blame Him or those around Him for whatever comes. When we walk outside of the umbrella of God, we are going to get weather. We can't dictate what kind.

And we certainly cannot walk in His authority if we are unwilling to die to our flesh (deny ourselves) daily and carry our cross. This means we must delight ourselves in the Lord by allowing His desires to become our desires; it is there that God will give us the desires of our heart. (See Matthew 16:24–25 and Psalm 37:4.)

Wherever we are in our journey, at some point, we are going to have to choose the Jesus who is free from the tomb. We are going to have to trust Him with what remains of our mess. We are going to have to behave like we are actually operating in resurrection power instead of throwing the stone from the tomb at someone else to cause injury. When Jesus walked out of the tomb, there was a grand display of resurrection power.

In *Homiletics and Hermeneutics*, Kenneth Langley writes:

> The Film maker Walt Disney was ruthless in cutting anything that got in the way of a story's pacing. Ward Kimball, one of the animators for Snow White, recalls working 240 days on a 4 1/2 minute sequence in which the dwarfs made soup for Snow White and almost destroyed the kitchen in the process. Disney thought it was funny, but he decided the scene stopped the flow of the picture, so out it went.
>
> When the film of our lives is shown, will it be as great as it might be? A lot will depend on the multitude of "good" things we need to eliminate to make way for the great things God wants to do through us. It will greatly depend upon the choices we make(p. 81).

If authority is found where identity is maintained and if identity is sealed through relational efforts toward Christ and obedience to Him, then if we are not spending time with Jesus and allowing Him to be in charge, we fail.

Jonah remembered his God and was delivered from the angry, hungry fish; he was violently spewed out on the shore, miles away, but nevertheless, free! Gideon remembered his God after he began to worship. He worshiped his God for being the conqueror because he finally believed He was. When David was in trouble—and he was often in a lot of trouble—he would sit down and repent and remember his God.

Deliverance comes, battles are won and victory happens when we remember our God. *Remembering Him is to go beyond what He does and remember who He is.* (See Psalm 103:7–13 and Exodus 13:3.)

We will never understand the fullness of our authority in Christ if we don't get Him out of the manger, take Him down from the Cross, and release Him from the tomb.

Today we must find a way to get past our trials, difficulties and disappointments. Life can get so big. I know your heart is broken, but so was His, and look what He was able to do!

We need to completely fall in love with Jesus again and again, allowing Him to be all in all, taking us with Him as He storms the enemy's camp and brings us an abundant life with perfect authority.

Doing so will create a sanctification in you that the enemy cannot touch, but it takes trust. You cannot fully love someone if you don't trust that person.

Three examples of the foundation of Christian living (to know, prefer and repent) are found in the lives of the centurion, Simeon and the jailor.

The centurion came running when he had a sick servant. This is a man who walked past hope into believing and set believing aside to walk in the knowing. By the time he came to Jesus, he wasn't hoping He could do it or believing that He might, *but knowing He would do it* for him, and therein lies the difference between relationship and fellowship with Jesus. (See Matthew 8:5–13.) One hopes. One knows and even expects.

Simeon carried the cross up to Calvary. He carried the very burden of the Lord, which is what we are to do. The design, desire and heart of Jesus Christ is pulsing upon the earth from Heaven to be glorified. Simeon preferred Jesus to the pain. (Many people run foolishly, chasing glitter and feathers, which are found in wild and false manifestations. These are not miracles; they are foolishness.)

We are to settle down and carry His burden across the nations, and *here we must live as we prefer Christ above and beyond ourselves* even if we feel as unable or as uncalled as Simeon. (See Luke 23:26.) Apparently, he was closer than the disciples who were "afar off," yet he was not a follower of Christ. Try to figure that out!

The jailor shouted with a desperate break in his soul to Paul, "What must I do to be saved?" It was *the embrace of his repentance that the Lord came upon.* He and his entire household were saved unto Christ. (See Acts 16.)

These men understood the *power of knowing, preferring and repenting*, which is the three-cornered platform of successful Christianity. If you don't have these, there are some failures that are chasing you down.

Our strength is directly determined by the amount of our weakness that we have given over to God.

Often, we cling to the "wrong Jesus" because we are too beat down to imagine that we are worthy to walk out of the tomb with Christ. Ephesians 3:19 says, "And to know the love of Christ that surpasses knowledge, that you may be filled with all the fullness of God."

According to *Today in the Word* from February 17, 1993,

> Race car driver, Bill Vukovich, won the famed Indianapolis 500 race in 1953 and 1954, a record of success few other drivers had matched. Asked the secret of his success in Indianapolis, Vukovich replied, "There's no secret. You just press the accelerator to the floor and steer left. Stick with the fundamentals."

To that end, I give you the fundamentals!

Acceptance, Security and Importance

The three keys to walking in freedom are: 1) you are accepted; 2) you are secure; and 3) you are important. As you come to understand these three keys, doubt will leave, and you will know you belong to the One. These are the fundamentals from which most personal successes spring.

1. I am accepted.

John 15:15

No longer do I call you servants, for the servant does not know what his master is doing; but I have called you friends, for all that I have heard from my Father I have made known to you.

2. I am secure.

Romans 8:31–34

What then shall we say to these things? If God is for us, who can be against us? He who did not spare his own Son but gave him up for us all, how will he not also with him graciously give us all things? Who shall bring any charge against God's elect? It is God who justifies. Who is to condemn? Christ Jesus is the one who died—more than that, who was raised—who is at the right hand of God, who indeed is interceding for us.

3. I am important.

2 Corinthians 5:17–21

Therefore, if anyone is in Christ, he is a new creation. The old has passed away; behold, the new has come. All this is from God, who through Christ reconciled us to himself and gave us the ministry of reconciliation; that is, in Christ God was reconciling the world to himself, not counting their trespasses against them, and entrusting to us the message of reconciliation. Therefore, we are ambassadors for Christ, God making his appeal through us. We implore you on behalf of Christ, be reconciled to God. For our sake he made him to be sin who knew no sin, so that in him we might become the righteousness of God.

———————————— ✦ ————————————

"Self-seeking is the gate by which a soul departs from peace while total abandonment to the will of God is the way by which it returns."

—Madame Jeanne Guyon
#51, *Gems*, late 1600s

———————————— ✦ ————————————

CHAPTER FIVE

Identity Dictates Behavior

"Identity is found where Time is spent. Authority is found where you have gained your Identity. Identity in Christ brings Authority in Christ."

—Donny Querin
Personal letter, 2010

U nforgiveness is an issue that comes against our identity in Christ probably more than anything else. It hinders our ability to do God's work and is generally rooted in three things: bitterness, fear and anger.

- *Bitterness* is blaming others, which then creates doubt.
- *Fear* of getting hurt again leads to a lack of trust. You can hold an inordinate fear of losing your pain and grief and actually create scenarios to hold onto them. Why? you have learned to manage them and almost feel safe held within the trauma.
- *Anger* makes you a frustrated, negative person, and now your identity is in your anger.

Whatever unforgiveness you deem justified, whatever wound you hold onto, will interfere with your identity in Christ. You can be sure that whatever is troubling you will rise up as you try to serve God. You pull it out by an act of your will within the Holy Spirit. Don't wait for the enemy to rise up to blindside you.

The enemy tries to keep us wounded and fearful so we will be ineffective in building God's Kingdom. He can do this easily if we are too consumed with ourselves. This can happen emotionally and physically.

Our physical or emotional diagnosis can be a terror we cling to: out of a fear of getting well and losing that identity, or out of a fear of not getting well and staying sick forever.

Sickness is often a part of where we have been, and we get used to catering to it: "I can't do it because I have this disease or sickness." Don't get me started on pushing through disease and sickness. Get up and stop it!

Phillip Yancey, in *What's So Amazing About Grace*, told this story:

> In 1862, Leo Tolstoy thought he was getting his marriage off on the right foot when he asked his teenage fiancé to read his diaries, which spelled out in lurid detail all of his prior immoral dalliances. He wanted to keep no secrets from Sonya, to begin marriage with a clean slate, forgiven. Instead, Tolstoy's confession sowed the seeds for a marriage that would be held together by vines of hatred and bitterness, not love.
>
> She would say with regret and a heavy heart, "I am always thinking, 'I'm not the first woman he has loved.'" This thought would overcome her for her whole life.
>
> Sonya Tolstoy would revisit this thought often in her own diary. Some of his adolescent flings from decades gone by she could forgive, but not his affair with Axinya, a peasant woman who continued to work on the Tolstoy estate.
>
> "One of these days I shall kill myself with jealousy," Sonya wrote after seeing the three-year-old son of the peasant woman, who was the spitting image of her husband.
>
> Another diary entry dates from January 14, 1909 in her later years, "He relishes that peasant wench with her strong female body and her sunburnt legs. She allures him just as powerfully now as she did all those years ago…"
>
> Sonya wrote those words when Axinya was a shriveled crone of more than 85.
>
> For half a century jealousy and unforgiveness had blinded her, and in the process destroying all the love she ever had for her husband (p. 85).

Sonya Tolstoy's identity became one of anger and hatred because she would not forgive. The truth became a lie because her soul had become completely dysfunctional.

Keeping track of a list of wrongs, complaining, finding justification in faults and rehashing wrongs to justify ourselves leads to complaining and bitterness.

When we need justification, we won't find justice.

For our time together here, go ahead and reconcile within yourself that many things in life don't appear to be fair and just don't make sense. Trust God anyway. Through this process, He will reveal His love to you in greater degrees.

Seeking justification for our wounds creates offense and leads to unbelief. When you have these in your life, they become your default. Then, when something bad happens, you automatically respond with bitterness, fear or anger instead of a Godly form of kindness toward those hurting you, which is trusting the Lord.

Trusting the Lord allows us to find joy through the trial because that helps us to "keep our eyes on the high calling of God in Christ Jesus," just as Jesus kept the cross ever before Him. (See Philippians 3:13–14 and Hebrews 12:2.)

Our identity in Christ is a lifetime quest. To begin our foundation, there are three things that we must endeavor to understand: 1) cause; 2) forgiveness; and 3) repair.

> *Even the mystery which hath been hid from ages and from generations, but now is made manifest to his saints: to whom God would make known what is the riches of the glory of this mystery among the Gentiles; which is Christ in you, the hope of glory* (Colossians 1:26–27 KJV).

What is the hope of glory in verse 27, and why does the whole of eternity brought down to the earth seem to hinge on it?

Having the hope of glory means that when people look at our lives, when they experience us or encounter us in any way, our lives should display Christ in a praiseworthy fashion in all that we do.

The fruit of the Spirit tucked in our soul becomes a very tangible reality. It is like a tree with ripe fruit—our fruit must be pickable. Not only that, but it also means that the people around us should anticipate with great joy, confidence and expectation that they will have this encounter with us and that they should look forward to it.

It means that we have not hidden Christ by our behavior.

We are the hope of the world because in us they see Jesus. We cannot get to that point unless we not only know who Christ is in us, but also who we are in Him. Is our salvation hinged upon what we have been "saved from," or does our salvation have a strong foundation and understanding of who we have been "saved into"? There is a striving for survival in one, while the other abides in a hope that passes all understanding.

An article from *Psychosomatic Medicine* told how, in 1957, researchers led by Dr. Curt Richter performed an experiment to see the effect that hope has on those undergoing hardship. Two sets of laboratory rats were placed in separate tubs of water.

The researchers left one set in the water and found that within an hour they had all drowned. The other rats were periodically lifted out of the water and then returned. When that happened, the second set of rats swam for days.

It was determined that the rats swam not because they had been given a rest, but because they suddenly had hope that they would be rescued!

To be clear, the cause, forgiveness and repairing of altars as mentioned here are a daily process in our life. Thus, I offer you these as a starting place:

1. Cause
Jeremiah was a bit of a tortured soul when he forgot why he was born.

> *Lord, you tricked me, and I was fooled. You are stronger than I am. So you won. I have become a joke. Everyone makes fun of me all day long. Every time I speak, I shout. I am always shouting about violence and destruction. I tell the people about the message I received from the Lord. But this only brings me insults. The people make fun of me all day long. Sometimes I say to myself, "I will forget about the Lord. I will not speak anymore in his name." But then the Lord's message becomes like a burning fire inside me. It feels like it burns deep within my bones. I get tired of trying to hold the Lord's message inside of me. And finally, I cannot hold it in* (Jeremiah 20:7–9 ICB).

Then, in chapter 21, Jeremiah got right back to work, fulfilling the cause of his life to be God's mouthpiece to declare truth.

Jeremiah had a cause, and when he allowed himself to be overcome by it, he became angry and lonely. When he realized God alone matters and his cause was true, then he was restored.

When he was consumed by his gift, things went south, but when he remembered the call, he was renewed. The fire of God was in his bones and wouldn't let him go.

2. Forgiveness

> *Pardon, I beseech thee, the iniquity of this people according unto the greatness of thy mercy, and as thou hast forgiven this people, from Egypt even until now. And the Lord said, I have pardoned according to thy word: but as truly as I live, all the earth shall be filled with the glory of the Lord* (Numbers 14:19–21 KJV).

God's idea of forgiveness is modeled throughout His Word. He will never stop loving us and He will never stop forgiving us. Forgiveness is, by design, a two-way street that has no shortcuts or exits. However, we are asked to forgive others, and God will hold us to it; we choose which way it will go.

> *And when ye stand praying, forgive, if ye have ought against any: that your Father also which is in heaven may forgive you your trespasses* (Mark 11:25 KJV).

Forgiveness is a choice, not a miracle!

3. Repairing the Altars in Our Life

In 1 Kings 18:17–39, Elijah could have just prayed, and the fire of God would have come to destroy the priests of Baal, the altar of sacrifice and the servants of King Ahab. But he did not, and why he did not is noteworthy.

> *And Elijah said unto all the people, Come near unto me. And all the people came near unto him. And he repaired the altar of the LORD that was broken down* (1 Kings 18:30 KJV).

Before the anointing abides, before the power of God will rest on something, the broken-down places must be repaired. You need to fix your mess. Apologize. Forgive. Reconcile.

This altar was going to be caught on fire anyway; there was no other point for repair, except for it to be properly done and to make a clean and beautiful offering to the Lord. Doing so will cost you something. It is supposed to.

Find the altars in your life that need to be repaired. Repairing them may be worthless to you, but it is not worthless to God. A secret pain, a ruined relationship, a disappointment, unforgiveness, anger or an unresolved grief—these are just a few. This is an exercise worth doing throughout your life to "keep things clean."

If our identity is to be found in Christ, then we must behave as Christ did.

Jesus had no broken altars in His life. He was clean and whole. It is mandated upon us to understand our cause. But before that we must—and this is a strict requirement—forgive and repair the altars in our life. We must forgive and repair before we seek ministry or attempt to be effective in someone else's life.

Wounded people wound others, but that is not why we are here. If we cannot get the altars repaired and forgiveness dispensed, our causes will be fractured and our identity unaccomplished. Jesus loves us, but at that point, we are stuck.

"The future belongs to those who believe in the beauty of their dreams," Eleanor Roosevelt is credited with saying. "Nobody can make you feel bad about yourself without your permission."

First Peter 2:9 says that we are a royal priesthood, a chosen, holy people who have been called out of darkness into Christ's wonderful light. Nobody can make you come out of the light. You, yourself, are in charge of that. So we don't necessarily have an identity issue or a sin issue; rather, it is a *priesthood issue.*

I have seen and considered that the loss of hopes, dreams and expectations can cause us to pull away from our calling and not be able to trust God. When we begin to behave badly, we lose ourselves.

There are times when we have to stop and realize that we have become the worst version of ourselves. If that is you, I assure you, there is a way out here in these pages.

When we ask for mercy and we get grace, we can sometimes be disappointed.

Mercy is the unmerited favor of God. It is as if we "throw ourselves down at the mercy of the court." We don't have it coming, but it is handed to us. We deliberately messed this thing up, we knew it was wrong, and we did it anyway. So, we make a last-ditch effort and beg for mercy—a way out of the punishment that we deserve.

Grace is our inherited right and ability to behave as Jesus did, full of His character and the fruit of the Spirit. So, when Peter says to "grow in grace" or when Paul says that the Lord's "grace is sufficient for you," they are saying, "Be like Jesus, do what Jesus would do, and that will be good enough."

This is not to say that we are saved by works; we are not. But if we continue to not behave as Christ did and allow our armor to be dented and ill-fitting, then eventually we will not believe Christ is in us at all. Grace says, "Get up and go."

How we behave is what we believe. What we believe is the foundation of our identity.

Before He was born, the angel said, "Call his name JESUS, for he will save his people from their sins" (Matthew 1:21). This means that we are rescued and saved not only from sin, but also from the cause of it and the need for it.

Finding Jesus as the Savior from the penalty of our sin does not always mean that we acknowledge Jesus as the One with the power over sin. We have to come into the understanding sometimes of that power. We do not have to do those things anymore, and if we crave to, then it means that we have minimized Christ and the price He paid. It means that we are refusing our royal priesthood.

If we do not recognize Jesus as the One who rescues us from the penalty of sin *and* as the One who has overcome our *need to sin*, then we have no authority over the enemy or sin itself. This means that we will keep behaving as if we are unsanctified.

The Christian life was not meant to create a religion of alternating failure and victory over and over in a cycle of sin and repentance. Rather, it is meant to be a life filled with overcoming power and authority!

> *For if I build again the things which I destroyed, I make myself a transgressor* (Galatians 2:18 KJV).

—————————◆—————————

"Define yourself radically as one beloved by God. This is the true self. Every other identity is illusion."
—Brennan Manning
Abba's Child, 1994

—————————◆—————————

Old Kingdoms Die Hard

"How can you pull down strongholds of Satan if you don't even have the strength to turn off your TV?"
—Leonard Ravenhill
Revival God's Way, 1984

Now that you know you have spiritual authority and understand your identity, there is going to be a battle. That's just how things work. You cannot take it personally, for you have switched kingdoms. You serve a new King, and the old king and the old man are angry and want you back. (See Romans 6.)

The enemy is counting on you to not believe, let alone know, that you are set free from him. These tools—spiritual authority and identity—are here for you to use, to see the enemy coming and beat him at his own game.

A January 1992 article in *Bits & Pieces* shows the power of belief:

> For centuries people believed that Aristotle was right when he said that the heavier an object, the faster it would fall to earth. Aristotle was regarded as the greatest thinker of all time, and surely he would not be wrong.
>
> Anyone, of course, could have taken two objects, one heavy and one light, and dropped them from a great height to see whether or not the heavier object landed first. But no one did until nearly 2,000 years after Aristotle's death. In 1589 Galileo summoned learned

professors to the base of the Leaning Tower of Pisa. Then he went to the top and pushed off a ten-pound and a one-pound weight. Both landed at the same instant. The power of belief in the error was so strong, however, that the professors denied their eyesight. They continued to say Aristotle was right (pp. 22-23).

The three primary tactical weapons that the enemy uses against us are: 1) deception; 2) temptation; and 3) accusation. With these tactics, he tries to hold us hostage in the old kingdom.

I realize this book appears to be a textbook, but we perish without knowledge and vision. If you don't see what is coming for you, then more than likely you will miss it. It is my desire that you stay in the fight to the end as a mighty overcomer who conquers because of great courage. (See Hosea 4:6, Proverbs 29:18, Romans 8:37 and Joshua 1:9.)

The Bible tells us that we struggle not against flesh and blood, but against demonic forces. (See Ephesians 6:12.) To not understand that Christianity is a battlefield is to misunderstand what you have been saved into. As I have said earlier, some rejoice at being saved from this or that and neglect the greater cause of what they have been saved into: the cause of Jesus Christ in the Kingdom of God.

So, here is a look at the devil's playbook.

1. Deception

To deceive somebody means to make another person believe a lie or to create doubt in him or her. (Another word is *guile*.)

- When the enemy sends deception your way, it is an attempt to get you to fall into error by not only believing a lie, but also holding to it and setting it forth on others—thus doing the devil's work for him in infecting and affecting others.
- *Strongholds are built through deception.*
  - A stronghold is formed when deception takes hold in a person's mind. Strongholds spring up from roots, and roots are what you believe.
  - A stronghold is an incorrect thinking pattern that stems from believing something that is not true.

From the very beginning, Satan deceived Eve into believing that God's Word was not true. In Genesis 3:4, the devil told Eve that she would not surely die as God said she would in Genesis 2:17. She believed a lie. She should have turned and walked away, or better yet, ran.

2. Temptation
Temptation often follows deception.

- First, the enemy tells us, "You won't surely die!" and then makes the fruit on the forbidden tree look good to us.
- Once Eve accepted Satan's deception (his lie), the tree that she was not supposed to touch looked good.
- She was tempted (enticed) to sin because she allowed herself to first be deceived. And, of course, she took somebody with her. That is generally how it works.
- Temptation comes when we are enticed or encouraged to sin in one way or another.
- James 1:13–15 (NKJV) says, "Let no one say when he is tempted, 'I am tempted by God'; for God cannot be tempted by evil, nor does He Himself tempt anyone. But each one is tempted when he is drawn away by his own desires and enticed. Then, when desire has conceived, it gives birth to sin; and sin, when it is full-grown, brings forth death."

In Matthew 4, Jesus saw through Satan's deception and resisted every temptation by speaking God's Word. King David said, in Psalm 119:11 (KJV): "Thy word have I hid in mine heart, that I might not sin against thee." When the enemy tempts you, he's showing you the worm, but behind that worm is a hook. The Word of God helps you see the hook behind the worm.

3. Accusations
The devil is known as the accuser of the brethren. (See Revelation 12:10.)

- He is known to take a believer who has done an embarrassing or gross sin and continue to rub that in his or her face, beating that person down with guilt, shame and condemnation over his or her past. Romans 8:1 (NKJV) says, however, that "there is therefore now no condemnation to those who are in Christ Jesus, who do not walk according to the flesh, but according to the Spirit."

Accusation is the enemy coming at you for things you did that are covered by the blood of Christ through your redemption. He can do this by throwing bad thoughts into your mind or by using other people.

This is not false accusation by others; you are past that now and understand that those are just people trying to clip you as the devil uses them. They are of no consequence at this juncture; just let them go. Rather, the accusation I am referring to here is the enemy's attempt to make the dead man come alive and give life to your past error.

The devil will come to accuse you with actual horrible things, and if you do not know that you are redeemed and forgiven with the assurance of salvation, he can ruin you. As you embrace your identity in Christ, you will know no shame.

God has a specific will for each of us, but basically His purpose and desire is to be glorified in our lives. The Bible uses various terms to reinforce this principle.

In Romans 8:29a (NKJV), God's purpose is that we be conformed to the image of Christ: "For whom He foreknew, He also predestined to be conformed to the image of His Son." Why does God predestine us to be conformed to His image? It is to glorify Him. Our ultimate calling is to love Jesus.

Satan tempts us to sin in order to keep God from being glorified. We have an enemy who is intent on robbing God of His glory in our life. God is glorified when we are conformed to the image of Christ and live like Him instead of like ourselves or the enemy. The devil just wants a pawn to hurt God's heart. Don't let him.

If your Adversary knows you won't quit, he will get tired of trying.

Charles Swindoll, in *Living Above the Level of Mediocrity*, wrote:

> Verdi's opera "La Traviata" was a failure when it was first performed. But on the second run, the singers chosen for the leading roles were the best of the day, however, everything went wrong. The tenor had a cold and sang in a hoarse, almost inaudible voice. The soprano who played the part of the young and delicate, sickly heroine had gained a lot of weight and evidently was now one of the largest ladies on or off the stage. Even though she was old beyond her years, she was very healthy and loud.
>
> At the beginning of the Third Act when the doctor declares that consumption has wasted away the "frail, young lady" and she cannot live more than a few hours, the audience was thrown into a

> spasm of laughter, a state very different from what was necessary to appreciate the tragic moment and is the very thing that made the opera such a hit! (p. 182).

In this opera, I don't think anyone predicted the outcome, but they hung in there and were happily surprised at the turn of events. Our willingness and obedience will spoil the enemy's plan every time. As we keep our eyes on the Lord, even the seemingly foolish things work out for our good.

God is always working His plan. It is important to know how God will come to you to request and even require your participation in that plan. How does He work with you? This is a question every saint must answer honestly. You need to know so that you can be waiting for the nudge of the Holy Spirit. I have always felt that there are two types of people: Red Sea walkers and Jordan River crossers.

The Red Sea walkers hear the Lord, see the plan, obey and almost immediately the waters of destruction part and the walkers are over on the other side, dry and comfortable. The fish are probably jumping into their bags and offering themselves up for sushi. Their quest is to keep going and not let anyone stop them. There are many people who are willing to jump on board with the Red Sea walkers' plan, but they often stop the progress because of their opinions outside of God's plan.

Walkers must keep their eyes on what is in front of them, beyond those around them, for they can see it. It is a long, rough, cold and scary night, but then quickly there is a powerful and miraculous redemption. They will be spoken of for generations to come. Oh, the greatness of the Red Sea parting!

Their enemies have been swallowed up by the sea, and now they are facing a vast and long wilderness. Songs are always sung! (See Exodus 14.)

The Jordan River crossers hear the Lord, do not see the plan beyond the land, obey anyway and trudge through muddy, swollen, scary waters full of leeches and gross things that go bump in the night. The water parts after they step in the muddy water and they find dry land, but not until they fight off the ideals of their mind. It is a lonely journey because many do not have the constitution of faith to go that way. Most will say, "More power to you!" and wave the crossers on. They will watch from afar. People are often afraid to march in until the water parts.

The Jordan River crossers have to get muddy and wet and not lose their footing in the unsteady ground beneath them. Then, and only then, will the waters part and they find dry ground. They have to hope and believe far beyond their means.

When these cross over to the other side, they look like a train hit them. They are wet, smelly and exhausted. The "toll of rules" has exhausted them. "Do this, or you die!" "Don't do this, or you will die!" However, in all of it, they have counted the crossing as an extravagant and amazing journey. Their enemies are all around, but they are looking at the Promised Land. They will have to fight to secure it, but the Jordan crossing taught them how to fight. (See Joshua 3–6.) Through this obedience, walls fall down and cities are won.

The Jordan River crossers are often unable to see exactly how the Lord will complete His work beyond the river, but they have obeyed and are glad. Even in their state, they are ready to enter the King's court. The walls of Jericho will fall. Songs are rarely sung!

Often the Lord will dip you into both kinds of water, but you will have a predominant swimming hole. Once you know that, you can gear up and be ready. Once you know who you are, there is no resentment, fear or concern. You create a battle cry from within, and you should.

So often, the Lord has an extravagant gift on the other side of our "water." However, we must have the bravery to get out of our own way and the courage to walk in God's plan.

If we settle for that small faith item, that is all we will receive and thereby that is all we will be able to bless others with. That is all we will be able to occupy and have authority over. As we walk through the waters (trials, afflictions, heartache, etc.), we may stumble and imagine all kinds of horrors. But as we follow the life of Jesus, we find that as we keep our heart and mind on what is ahead of us, to God's glory, then we have peace. And with peace, we can do anything!

Redemption is not simply for our benefit. He saves us, redeems us, restores us to a relationship with Himself, gives us a new life in Christ, and fills us with His Spirit not exclusively for our blessing, but for His glory. Miracles flow there.

We have power to be His witness, without intimidation, because His presence is within us. Once we have been crucified with Christ, we no longer seek self-gratification or appreciation. Our identity, settled in Jesus Christ, will cause us to walk in an authority that will win every battle in the demonic realm and here on this earth.

You may wonder why that battle is so fierce. It is because we just happen to be in the middle of a feud that existed long before we showed up. You have to choose a side, whether you want to or not. You are in a fight; you might as well suit up.

Just a few short years before his death, Vance Havner, who became a revivalist and turned his denomination on its ear, said, when referring to the New Testament Church, that revival is "the saints going back to normal."

A lack of spiritual power is a lack of understanding dominion, which boils down to an authority issue.

When doubt arrives at the doorstep of our belief, there are all kinds of problems that come with it. If we allow doubt to wrap itself around what we believe, we become double-minded and unstable. (See James 1:8.) In that system, we can never forge our way through "hoping" to "knowing." Belief is supposed to act like a guide between those two elements, and if belief is crippled, then it cannot push us forward with any faith from simply hoping to absolutely knowing. Doubt is a terrible thing.

When we arrive with our identity intact, it becomes easy to dismantle the tactics of the enemy. He is deeply afraid of you understanding your authority in Christ. So, let's consider dominion and authority.

God gave man dominion. Man gave it to the enemy. Jesus gave authority to man to take the dominion back.

> *Then God said, "Let Us make man in Our image, according to Our likeness; let them have dominion over the fish of the sea, over the birds of the air, and over the cattle, over all the earth and over every creeping thing that creeps on the earth." So God created man in His own image; in the image of God He created him; male and female He created them. Then God blessed them, and God said to them, "Be fruitful and multiply; fill the earth and subdue it; have dominion over the fish of the sea, over the birds of the air, and over every living thing that moves on the earth"* (Genesis 1:26–28 NKJV).

> *So God blessed Noah and his sons, and said to them: "Be fruitful and multiply, and fill the earth. And the fear of you and the dread of you shall be on every beast of the earth, on every bird of the air, on all that move on the*

earth, and on all the fish of the sea. They are given into your hand" (Genesis 9:1–2 NKJV).

In both passages, we see God blessing them because that is what God does. But something has changed. In Genesis 1, they have dominion. In chapter 9, they don't. Instead of having dominion over the things on the earth, they now would only have the guarantee that the animals would fear them. That's it.

Man would have to wait for Jesus to take dominion back through His authority. (We own it and have the power to prove and enforce it. But do we know that?)

God gave man dominion in the Garden of Eden. While there, man gave it up to the enemy. He gave it away. He sold his birthright for a piece of fruit.

After the flood, God said to Noah, "I will make the creatures on the earth fear you." Mankind would fight and strive, struggle and wrestle, for all the generations that would come before Christ because they had no authority to take back dominion.

Mankind abounded only when the Spirit of the Lord came upon them, and even then it was only a select few. They did not have the privilege of the abiding presence of Jesus or the power of His Spirit, as we do.

When Jesus came, He gave us the authority to take the dominion back, to take what the locust and the cankerworm had eaten. (See Joel 2.) We are guaranteed complete restoration through Christ in all things—nothing left out, nothing lost, nothing broken. *We stand with Jesus Christ, enforcing the victory that was already secured at Calvary.*

If you have been a Christian longer than 5 minutes, then you are probably aware that there are forces of good and evil all around you. Remembering who you belong to will decide which side you occupy. You cannot wander over, it is a distinct decision that must be made from the core of your soul, where the knowing lies. This decision is on purpose with no looking back.

You have been given a destiny to go forward, to change things. You have been given a calling that will embrace every difficult situation and as they say "Spit in the wind," for the goals God has laid upon you. There is no shrinking back in you. There is no confusion about what Kingdom you belong to. You have been given permission to speak and be heard. The earth is waiting as all of heaven rejoices over the decision you are making.

Remember, faith is a mountain.... Climb it!

———————————— ✦ ————————————

"The devil has no authority over any Christian, except the authority we grant him by believing him."

—Jon Bloom
"How Satan Gets a Hold on You," 2018

———————————— ✦ ————————————

CHAPTER SEVEN

The Last Stronghold

"Sanctification is the work of the Holy Spirit in us whereby our inner being is progressively changed, freeing us more and more from sinful traits and developing within us over time the virtues of Christlike character."

—Jerry Bridges

To destroy the last stronghold, we must deal with incorrect mindsets. These strongholds live in our soul and are very hard to remove because we are used to them abiding there and we protect them. They have become part of our personality.

I want to specifically first address the victim mentality, as I feel like this is one of the strongest things that people hold on to in error. It often is the very last stronghold to leave. It is as strong as a demonic possession, a far-reaching oppression.

Some people call this mentality strange "spiritual" names (Jezebel, Python.....) and try to get people to "break free" from it when the truth is, it is a learned and harbored behavior and must be dealt with from a practical and persistent pursuit. Basically, you are, I am—the self—is the last stronghold, and it must be taken down for the sake of freedom in Christ.

When our pain has been allowed to maintain real estate in our soul for a length of time, it becomes part of our personality, and we force every part of our life and those around us to bow to it. We play the tune in our heads repeatedly until it forms the sentence we can often live by when we have unreconciled wounds: "I am miserable; therefore, this is who I am." Over time, our feelings can become substitutes for love and acceptance, and we protect them even if their names are sickness, victim, rejection, abandonment and forsaken. The visitors list just goes on and on.

Because this is such a harmful and huge issue, I want to spell out a few, somewhat clinical, notes so that you may gain a better understanding here.

When you are set free to love Jesus, you often have the garbage of your former life left to deal with. Your spirit got saved, not your body, soul and mind; they need work. Many ailments are given as "a gift" from childhood. Perhaps you were not listened to as a kid; you were never heard, never seen, yet always blamed. This is a recipe for disaster, beyond other types of abuses.

Most people who have needed deliverance of some sort or another were mishandled as children, and that often causes them to seek out relationships later in life that reinforce the error. Familiar spirits seek their own. When this happens, the brain gets busy creating avenues of survival. Part of the need to be accepted in this will come as the need to serve.

If a person is "put to work" in the Kingdom too soon, he or she gets buried under all the servanthood and desire to be accepted and will never be well. At that point, the victim's heart finds a purpose.

A victim mentality is an acquired personality trait in which a person tends to recognize him or herself as a victim because of the negative actions of others, either real or imagined, toward him or her. The person behaves as if this were the case even in the face of clear evidence to the contrary.

Because the individual's personality is wrapped up in being a victim, it is very difficult for the person to simply function and believe nobody wants to hurt them. Or worse yet, the victim will find it impossible to believe that they are okay. Almost every scenario will be about them as they defend and protect their right to be a victim and unwell. If the emotional work isn't done, then even after a mighty deliverance, they remain afflicted, but at that point, it is not the enemy, it is they, themselves, the last stronghold.

If I am sitting at a table and three other people happen to come by and sit down, uninvited by me, and seat themselves in the remaining three chairs at the table, a fourth person also may come by and, if that person wants to sit, then they will. If the person doesn't, they won't. Nobody really thinks past these things. Furthermore, nobody really cares. Or one shouldn't.

However, if the fourth person is easily offended, that individual probably has a victim mentality. If that is the case, the victim will say that he or she was not invited to the table. The victim will not listen when I say, "I didn't invite these people; it is not a secret party." It doesn't matter how patiently I endeavor to explain that *nobody was invited, they were not left out,* and *people simply sat in chairs.*

That person will spend a great deal of time feeling bad about something that didn't happen and blaming others for an invisible offense. This deception creates a need to gossip and tell others of the unfair behavior that was exhibited against him or her. If there is nothing for the person to be offended about, then the victim will be offended for someone else or create an offense based on falsehood and spread that around so they can have a platform of "pain."

Victim mentality is primarily developed from family members and social situations during childhood. Children often learn this mentality from parents who model it for them. I have seen children misdiagnosed with emotional ailments simply because they were mimicking their parents' behavior. Some parents gain an identity out of their sick children and there is no talking them out of it, even when the children become well.

Similarly, criminals often engage in victim thinking, believing themselves to be righteous, operating in their own moral code. They are engaging in crime only as a reaction to an immoral world. Furthermore, they feel that police are unfairly singling them out for persecution. They generally feel that crime and addiction are okay for them because they must deal with what error lurks in their soul.

Victim mentality is generally set in a child from something that happened to that child that was validly unjust or unfair and not handled correctly. Children come to parents for affirmation and rescue, for comfort and encouragement. Often, in an effort to teach a child, a dictator's attitude will come out of the parent and break the child's spirit. At that point, the child is open to all kinds of emotional disasters. Such children often spend their lives blaming others for their trauma and do not take ownership of their problems.

When a child has been wronged or harmed and the parent does not effectively rescue that child, it puts a seed of "victim" thinking in him or her because "nobody will hear me or help me." This can happen at one instance (which would mean that the child is predisposed to this condition, and it is generational or spiritual) or from many things happening over and over where the child was not heard or rescued and caused to bear the blame for something they did not do.

This situation can bring individuals to live in a perpetual state of frustration, disappointment, anxiety, worry, anger and hate because they feel they are owed something. Frustration and anger build up based on the fear that they will never be rescued or heard, and therefore they must rescue themselves. That is when the games really begin. It is difficult if not impossible to get them to trust...ever. But God....

Strangely enough, at any age, over a period of time when such people are shown empathy and fearful situations are removed from their lives, they experience a cure to the victim mentality. Acting out is often a cry for help, and as a person knows he or she can receive empathy, can be rescued and can be vindicated, that person will become soothed and actually begin to see him or herself beyond the victim and stop acting out altogether.

A Christian family must be particularly careful about hypocrisy. Children see this hypocrisy, and it wreaks havoc on their souls. I see this damage over and over, and I would say it is the number one reason children of Christian homes spin out. Maybe it was something small; maybe it was large. Either way, apologies are needed.

This mentality bleeds back to identity and acceptance. If a person feels like they are not accepted by God and have no identity in Him, that person will seek out identity and especially acceptance from others, as I have said.

Victory at the Battle of Bennington in Vermont was gained, it is said, because a little lame boy, an apprentice of the local blacksmith, who was out of town, set a shoe on Colonel Warren's tender-footed horse, which enabled the colonel to lead his regiment just in time to save the day. The victory of Bennington decided the Battle of Saratoga, which decided the Revolutionary War. Praise God for a little lame boy who was not afraid of his physical limitations and refused to "live" there. This boy refused to be a victim. He refused to be defined by his ailment, so he was able to do a great thing.

As we play the victim, we are unable to build the Kingdom of God. Instead, we will actually tear it down, desperate to be vindicated from old, worn-out, wrinkled wounds.

Beyond victimism, the victim mentality can develop into two separate disorders that greatly complicate recovery:

1. **Victim Syndrome** – Here a person displays passive aggressive behavior and often is afraid to be alone.
2. **Passive Victims** – These are people whose fear creates anger. Although they have never really been victimized, they often are offended about someone else's trial and are afraid they might have one themselves— (sort of a "victim's heart in advance, just in case.")

As you can see, one might be taught to be a victim as a child or even adopted the idea of being a victim as an adult. If we are not anchored to the Cross, this victim's heart will not be extinguished. When the victim's heart is allowed to rule our life, it destroys our ability to put the devil in his place.

We cannot thrive in Christ and arrive at sanctification when we have given this last stronghold a place to rent in our soul. And that really is the point—these things don't own us; they are renting. They are waiting to be kicked out.

Alternatively, the creator mindset allows people to appropriate correct decisions for any given situation, responding correctly among many choices, having viewed the entire situation. They are ready and willing to serve others in the solution.

The enemy must be cast down and taken out because, more than likely, if you have operated in the victim mindset, you have given him this ground. You must take it back if you are to be one who proclaims the good news of Jesus as a fearless Herald. At first, maybe it was just you carrying on. But, as time goes by and you fold into this mindset, you give the enemy permission to own it.

Switching the victim mentality to the creator mindset can be done and needs to be done. You must admit errors and choose to be different. Accountability is incredibly important at this juncture.

When you choose to be different, you can be at liberty to change your responses. This *is* something you can do because the Lord will help you do it. But it takes the practice of purposeful behavioral modification.

I have found that the Holy Spirit speaks the most truth to us when we are willing to be wrong.

Every stimulus requires a choice, and that choice will go one of two ways: either the person chooses the victim mindset (blaming, accusing, making excuses, overreacting) or the creator mindset (seeking solutions before reacting, taking action by trying something new).

A Focus on the Family article by Carlene Mattson says this:

> The greatest obstacle to being handicapped—or challenged, or disabled or whatever label we may be using this year—is not the condition but the stigma society still associates with it. The truth is we are valuable because of who we are, not because of how we look or what we accomplish. And that applies to all of us, the disabled and the temporarily able-bodied alike.
>
> I'm convinced God didn't turn His back at the moment of Jeff's conception. He is still the God of miracles, but in this instance, the one who received healing was me. Our Lord is still in the business of changing lives, but not always in the ways we expect. Several years ago, Jeff played in a special Little League for kids with disabilities.
>
> After many seasons of watching from the bleachers and rooting while his big brother played ball, Jeff's opportunity finally arrived. When he received his uniform, he couldn't wait to get home to put it on. When he raced out from his bedroom, fully suited up, he announced to me, "Mom, now I'm a real boy!" Though his words pushed my heart to my throat, I assured him he had always been a real boy (p. 13).

Worthlessness is a root. It is something you believe. It is different than unworthiness, which is situational and may come and go as a stronghold branch (how you process what your root tells you that you are). To consider yourself worthless means that you feel as if there is not a place of redemption for you, that this is who you are, worthless.

Worthlessness can become a core belief while unworthiness is able to be fought off with our identity in Christ. Unworthiness can be fixed in a day, even a moment. Worthlessness can shout at you from beneath your soul and become a root. The belief system in our roots need to be transformed to what God thinks about us and not what the world thinks. (See Romans 12:2.)

When you see yourself as having your worth in Jesus Christ, you begin to understand identity and redemption. When worthlessness goes away and the root dies, so will the branch of unworthiness that keeps popping up everywhere for almost no reason at all. You are born free in Christ, so live free in Him.

Life is made up of many choices that come from the cycle of identity. It will make you a victim or an overcomer. It is in this tight circle of belief (what you hold to be true), response (emotional) and reaction (physical) that this battle is fought and won.

Consequences to responses and reactions will either confirm or deny what you believe.

This cycle can be good or bad, and it is never-ending in our lives. Do the best you can, and that will be enough, for God is hard at work as we are faithful in the little laid before us.

You may stay in a dead-end job because you think that is all you are destined for. You may stay in a frightful marriage because that is all you think you are worth. Perhaps you will refuse to risk anything because you are afraid to lose. The excuses pile up and become reasons.

When you get there, you begin to guilt yourself into believing that "this is all there is, and I should suffer through it because there is no hope." Then you can suffer the possibility that you are a victim, and you will self-sabotage yourself by purposefully making bad decisions to ensure that you will fail. *In the end, you blame God that He wasn't faithful; then you don't trust Him and are at risk of doubting that He even exists.*

The bad news is, there is a wickedness at the core of that thinking. Maybe we inherited it somehow or life itself taught us it. But now is the time to break free from it. Tell the devil to *go* and ask the Lord to *come*.

Afterwards, practice making great decisions that follow the peace of God. Find a friend to help you out along the way because, by now, making dumb choices has probably become a habit.

We often find, in our quest to uncover sacred truth, that we, ourselves, all along, have been the worst stronghold to ever come upon our lives. We manipulate to survive and it becomes a lifestyle. We negotiate around truth to be able to cope. We deceive ourselves so we can endure. Then, it happens to us, not quickly, but ever so slowly... we have become the tools that we used to deal with our lives.

But the Lord has deemed you worthy for so much more. I did not come speaking smooth words and you did not come to hear them. Instead, you are ready, ready for truth and change.

Because the real meaning of Revival is change. Things have to change and the change must begin with us. This is how the Road to Sanctification is marched... not walked or limped along, but marched. It is a good day to leave where you were to get where you are going.

———————————— ✦ ————————————

"Deliverance from believing lies must be done by believing truth."

—Jessie Penn-Lewis
War on the Saints, 1912

———————————— ✦ ————————————

CHAPTER EIGHT

The Herald

"There is no worse enemy to your freedom and your peace of mind than the undisciplined affections of your own heart."
—Thomas à Kempis
The Imitation of Christ, 1450

A
s we leave behind what pulls us back and holds us down, we find that we are on a glorious road; we see that the paragraph in our life is more than a mere sentence.

This paragraph will teach us and help us, by continued choices toward the Cross, to prefer Christ, and that is when we begin to walk away from "normal" and find ourselves, with the help of God Himself, fit for His own use in many peculiar ways.

It takes this process of change to win in battle. As we shed ourselves of ourselves, we realize this is where we know the difference between what we want and what the Lord wants.

It takes a sanctified person who fears no one but God and who hates nothing but sin to proclaim the message of the Forerunner, the one who is a Herald.

Knowing that we are of a royal priesthood—beyond called, but chosen—helps us to push through the process every journey will take us on. This is the journey that leads us from purification to consecration and onward into sanctification. It will always require the denial of our flesh so the Holy Spirit can fully occupy our soul beyond our spirit. It is a lifelong quest, a beautiful journey.

65

We will always win the battle that is the Lord's because He has ordained it and prepared a way out of it or through it. (See 1 Corinthians 10:13.) The battles we design are different; they are drawn with our own desires and have no image of God in them. They are those He cannot and should not honor.

God's heart is for salvation upon the earth; it is for the reviving of those who are called by His name. When Jesus is lifted high, walking in His love and power becomes a lifestyle.

Jesus destroys darkness. He obliterates it. That is what Calvary did. Jesus did not become the resurrected Savior so we could rent that party boat on the weekends. He did not become the resurrected Savior so we could dress up in Halloween costumes and celebrate a satanic event. He did not become the resurrected Savior so we could be gloriously accepted and applauded by the world.

Jesus loves you, but He didn't die and rise again so that you could be comfortable. He did that so you would know the Father and know His love. Held within that love should be a desire to please Him beyond yourself, and that is where the rub comes for some.

Denial of self is where some quit because they have made themselves important, too important, sitting on a throne, judging and condemning all who would selflessly do the work.

Be careful what you imagine for yourself. Get in or get out; a fence straddler is only trouble and a heartache to those who are searching to know Christ fully.

Judas was a fence straddler until he fell off completely onto the wrong side of the fence. I think he felt that he could enjoy both sides until the devil came and told him one day that he, the devil, had ownership of that fence!

A military force generally works by two fundamental standards: *numbers and training.*

When only half of the army is available because the soldiers lose their push, the other half suffers, and so does the work. The other half, the faithful half, must wait or push beyond their limits into an apparent collapse.

For those who remain, they must be trained so that an implosion is not imminent. This training brings power to the waiting, and it is my hope and desire that the things written to you here will train you up to travel the way you should go.

Battle lines are being drawn, shots have been fired, and the waiting is just about over. God will use what He has. He will empower those who are faithful and have lost their own agenda and identity to His.

He will equip them with His own glory as they honor Him. These are the believers who allow Christ to be the Lord in their surrendered and yielded life. These are the believers who say, "Christ in me, the hope of glory." (See Colossians 1:27.)

You are reading this book, so I believe you are done with the struggle of your flesh and are ready to yield fully to the Lord. I believe you are ready to go gain for Christ His victory of saints redeemed. Even beyond that, you are looking to present a spotless bride to the Lord, which is the greatest gift we could ever endeavor to present.

It is time to pick up the torch and run. Finish taking those grave-clothes off and kick aside that heavy rock that has barred you in the tomb of your own fear and despair. It is truly time to "run your race," as the apostle Paul has said. Many of us have tasted and know it is true, while some have simply spied on the battlefield from afar.

Remember that God will do the work in each of us for His glory as we surrender to Him. He always does the heavy lifting; you can count on that.

You will find your surrender song here in these pages as the melody turns into a battle cry in the midst of a victory march.

Pain, trauma, grief and trials are a real part of life. We should take the time needed to tend to those things and allow the precious Holy Spirit to powerfully, yet gently, bathe our soul in the beauty that only He can bring.

As Ecclesiastes 3 says, there is a time for everything. There is a time to heal, a time to mourn and a time to go into battle. Heal well, my friend, and then go on to the victory.

No treasured saint of old ever became greatly effective for the Kingdom of God from a lawn chair constantly ministering to their own wounds. How long will your wounds of church hurt, betrayal, abandonment and so many other things (valid and terrible things) hold you hostage to their pain?

Often, when we linger in the pain, we create scenarios that never happened and increase the terror. This allows the enemy to own even more real estate in our mind and soul. Simmered pain does that. Like a stew, it grows and grows in the flavor that is in the pot as it sits.

How long has your pot been simmering? Warriors for Christ get well and get up. And in case you are wondering, we are all warriors, for we are engaged in a battle. We will operate differently, but we are at war with an enemy, following the directive of our Commander-in-Chief, Jesus Christ.

Sometimes, more often than not, we *are* well, but the enemy rushes in to convince us that we are weak and traumatized and need increasingly more help. We find others who are good at CPR of the soul, and they keep telling us that we are barely making it: "Sit here and be ministered to." Poor trauma-bound you is held captive by those who have a need outside of Christ to keep you weak so they can feel that they are of use. It's an identity crisis.

These people build a following, a club of fools that they can manipulate into pain. They are the fabricators of stories that never happened and of pain that was so minimal it would have barely been acknowledged if forgiveness and mercy were dispensed quickly with grace, according to Scripture. (See Matthew 18:15–17 and 2 Corinthians 13:1–3.)

While the band plays on and the army marches by, these who operate in this terror sit in disgrace, blaming others for their drama. They never do a thing to grow the Kingdom of God because they are just too big themselves—bigger than Christ. Sickening.

It is not that you are unimportant; it's just that you are not more important than Jesus and what He is trying to accomplish on this earth for the Father's glory. I guess, if He has to go about using donkeys again, He will. But how entirely sad for the state of the Church at large if that is the truth.

Deliverance shouts from the soul of the human frame as a needy child who will be satisfied with nothing less than the fulfillment of their desire to be fully free, redeemed and delivered of itself. Jesus holds every part of redemption in His hand, and His hand is so beautifully upon you. It's just that there is that simmering pot....

As I was pondering these things for you, I began to remember some things I was shown as a teenager about the Herald. God told me to walk that way and not look back.

The definition of herald (according to *Merriam-Webster's Dictionary*) to tuck into your soul is this: "An official crier or messenger. One that precedes or foreshadows. One that conveys news or proclaims: announcer. One who actively promotes or advocates."

> *Behold, I send My messenger, and he will prepare the way before Me. And the Lord, whom you seek, will suddenly come to His temple...* (Malachi 3:1 NKJV).

In preparation for a great visitation, God may raise up many messengers, each preparing the way of the Lord in their own appointed spheres. This is surely a day when God is looking for Heralds to blaze the trail of restoration and renewal in Him. These are not smooth preachers, but rugged prophets: saints with the stamp of Elijah, who, with the hand of the Lord upon him, girded up his loins and ran before the king to the entrance of the royal city. (See 1 Kings 18:46.) Thus Elijah demonstrated the spiritual work that he was doing as a Herald.

On Mount Carmel, Elijah had prepared the way of the Lord, and now the Lord was coming "as the latter and former rain" that "water the earth." (See Hosea 6:3 and Psalm 72:6.) As God calls us out from the world, we must be prepared for a pathway of unpopularity and misunderstanding. "You troubler of Israel" was the way Ahab addressed Elijah. (See 1 Kings 18:17.) So this prophet whom God had sent to deal with the "Achans in the camp" was himself accused of being one. (See Joshua 7:25.)

John the Baptist also demonstrates this element in the ministry of the Herald. Standing alone as the Champion of righteousness, he unmasked the hypocrisy of the religionists and even denounced the sin of the king upon the throne.

This man, who was "much more than a prophet," was called to seal his ministry with his own blood, and thereby he succeeded in preparing the way of the Lord. (See Matthew 11:11.)

The Herald prepares the way of the Lord and knows that it is not a popularity contest. The first and last component to this effort is to have a clean heart and soul. Whether it is to pray or serve others, to stand up against injustice or speak volumes of truth, a Herald will see to it.

From The Rule of St. Benedict, Sixth Century A.D.
If any pilgrim monk come from distant parts, with wish as a guest to dwell in the monastery, and will be content with the customs which he finds in the place, and do not perchance by his lavishness disturb the monastery, but is simply content with what he finds, he shall be received, for as long a time as he desires.

If, indeed, he find fault with anything, or expose it, reasonably, and with the humility of charity, the Abbot shall discuss it prudently, lest perchance God has sent him for this very thing.

But, if he have been found contumacious (argumentative or controversial) in the time of his sojourn as a guest, not only ought he not be joined to the body of the monastery, but also it shall be said to him, honestly, that he must depart. If he does not go, let two stout monks, in the name of God, explain the matter to him.

Even when "stout monks" chase you down, you must be true to the One who sent you.

The Herald must be one who can say, as Micah did, "But truly I am full of power by the spirit of the Lord, and of judgment, and of might, to declare unto Jacob his transgression, and to Israel his sin" (Micah 3:8 KJV).

Jeremiah was another one who was a called Herald. In a day dark with moral decline, his fearless ministry helped to check the evils of the time and prepare the way for a reviving that he did not live to witness, for it came under Ezra and Nehemiah. The commission given to him by the Lord is deeply significant.

> *See, I have set you this day over nations and over kingdoms, to pluck up and to break down, to destroy and to overthrow, to build and to plant* (Jeremiah 1:10).

It should be noted that there is twice the emphasis on the negative element as on the positive; two thirds of Jeremiah's ministry was to be destructive and only one third constructive. Truth-telling can do that.

Jeremiah was full of God's power in the middle of a powerful commission, but there were those who cried because he did not come with smooth words while destroying darkness and dismantling the plans of man.

Often, a characteristic of the work of one who is a Herald is that he or she will go against the flow, even in a disturbing manner at times. Stumbling blocks of iniquity have to be destroyed and stones of unbelief have to be thrown out if the way of the Lord is to be prepared. (See Isaiah 57:14; 62:10.) Heralds do their best to comply with the mannerisms of the court, but when push comes to shove, often the king has got to go!

The very word *prepare* contains this idea of casting out, emptying and clearing as a field before planting. An almost destructive, ruthless, yet thorough set of behaviors must precede the greater work of construction that is to follow. It will cost you.

Let God lead you and stop being afraid of losing the kind of people in your life who crucified Jesus. If you need to be celebrated instead of tolerated, then Christianity is not for you. Being called by Christ means to live like Christ.

Manna must go so *the new corn can come.*

If you are to operate as the Herald of God's heart, you must repent of your errors, not only to God, but also to those whom you damaged. Repair the altar, restore the breach and watch God put you into the game right there in center field. It will be a good day when that happens. The team is waiting for you.

> *For God so loved the world, that he gave his only begotten Son, that whosoever believeth in him should not perish, but have everlasting life. For God sent not his Son into the world to condemn the world; but that the world through him might be saved. He that believeth on him is not condemned: but he that believeth not is condemned already, because he hath not believed in the name of the only begotten Son of God. And this is the condemnation, that light is come into the world, and men loved darkness rather than light, because their deeds were evil. For every one that doeth evil hateth the light, neither cometh to the light, lest his deeds should be reproved. But he that doeth truth cometh to the light, that his deeds may be made manifest, that they are wrought in God* (John 3:16–21 KJV).

Remembering who you belong to, who paid an extravagant price for your heart, and who speaks directly into your destiny should gird your soul up with such bravery and courage that fear cannot live there. Then you will be free to march as you should, accomplishing every great goal Christ has set before you.

And with the end of this chapter, you have found your way through bravery and arrived in the land of courage to become a fearless Herald for the causes of Christ. I salute you.

Sometimes we become stuck in the wilderness where the desert gets a hold of us, and that is where we need to stay for a time. Crossing the Red Sea takes time and forces an incredible amount of patience upon us. The Jordan River crossing takes constant fearlessness that becomes actual faith. We emerge as our souls are made ready.

As you come to the end of this journey, you can surely see what a horrible liability it is to allow woundedness to occupy space in your soul even one more day. Lean on the Lord and trust Him; He will give you the strength to tell the devil *no* and help you back up your convictions with actions.

I am confident that as you pass through the elements of authority and identity and lean into your liberty in Christ that the enemy will fail in his quest to sabotage you with every mentality that rails against your spirit and your ability to overcome.

Becoming a Herald for Christ and His Kingdom is the most honored position we can hold. The Lord will fill you with His passion, zeal and very unction to accomplish incredibly hard things and you will just sail right through.

Accomplishing the purposes of the Lord will become second nature to you. The bystanders will continue to stand by and wonder what happened. You be you and let them be them. Be true to how the Lord has formed you through these pages and there will be no stopping you within His purposes. You will change your world for His honor and glory. That is what The Herald does.

May God bless you with every blessing as you go forward.

———————————— ✦ ————————————

"A fearful vessel will never perform the tasks of a Herald. Furthermore, it is possible to evade a multitude of sorrows by the cultivation of an insignificant life."

—John Henry Jowett
*"Come Ye Apart," Daily Exercises in Prayer
and Devotion,* 1920

———————————— ✦ ————————————

CHAPTER NINE

The Believers and the Bride

I leave you with a portion of a dream that the Lord gave me twenty-five years ago. It was given as a warning, and I find it relevant here.

It was autumn. I remember the leaves turning color, and what a beautiful sight that was, until it was not. Beauty gave way to a mess of leaves in mud. *Why does hope spring forth at all, just to have disaster devour it so often?* I remember thinking.

I am a wedding planner. It is a dream job until you have an important client and things get ahead of you. My client was the King, and this was to be His Son's wedding. His Son was paying for everything and didn't want His bride bothered with anything, so I had been working with Him more than with the bride.

As it turns out, the King was to officiate the wedding Himself. He was radiant somehow. I fell speechless around Him. He allowed His Son to do most of the managing of the details as He watched on with a caring and protective gaze.

His Son had so much love in His eyes when He looked at His bride; it was obvious to me that He adored her. What was about to happen to Him was clearly unfair and cruel. Yet, He stood waiting, I thought, unknowingly. He had no clue. But, somehow, looking back on what happened, I think He knew and just chose to wait...and wait.

The people in the congregation seemed to know the King, but they apparently never made the time to know His Son. It seemed to me that they were at the wedding out of some obligation or functionary purpose.

The people sat there judging the decorations, the chapel and each other. Because the ceremony was delayed, they had more time to misbehave, so they did.

It was my job to keep things sane and the schedule moving along. But, with every minute, my job grew more difficult as the congregation became more preoccupied with themselves.

The music was playing and everyone was in place, but where was the bride? Nobody knew where she was. I left the chapel to go on the hunt and found her. What a disgusting disgrace. She sat in a corner room, eating chocolate in her wedding gown.

Smears of chocolate stained the gown. She kept wiping her hands on her dress, and it just kept getting dirtier and dirtier. With every bite, she grew bigger and bigger, and her gown shrunk smaller and smaller.

I begged her to stop eating, but she wouldn't. She ignored me. I tried to clean the chocolate on the gown, and she pushed me away. "Let me help you!" I urged, to no avail. She was consumed with herself.

"This is your wedding day! Listen, don't you hear the wedding march playing? It's your song!" I tried to compel her to get up and go to her Groom. She wouldn't.

I tried to force her to move, then realized her gown was gapping in the back. She had outgrown her wedding gown by at least three sizes. She shrieked, "Get away from me! I don't want to hear it!"

She had become a sloppy mess, completely self-absorbed, and there was no way I could zip up her dress. I cried and pleaded with her. "Leave me alone," she waved her hand. "There is plenty of time." She was drowning in her own lust.

A large glass door was open from this room to the outside. She sat near the door and longed to be outside.

Her affection for the King and His Son had grown cold as she longed for other things.

People outside walking by waved at her and brought her food and sweets along with promises of pleasure in faraway places. They told her that she would be better off doing something else. And, like Eve entertaining a snake, she listened.

These people comforted her with cheap words and cheap treats. They began to tell her that she was not ready to be married or committed to someone else, that there was still so much more for her to experience in this wonderful life, unfettered with no responsibility.

I closed the glass door, but she opened the window. The wanderers outside seized the opportunity and began showing her magic tricks and talking about a life away from this place of responsibility and upheld honor. They began playing games with her and talking about all the fun they would have.

What they didn't tell her is that those things also mean one is un-protected—unsafe with a dead destiny.

As people were jumping around like circus clowns and fortune tell-ers, throwing glitter and acting out foolishness, five women stopped and began to talk to the bride. "No," I told her, "you must get cleaned up; your Groom is waiting." I had recognized these women.

These were the women whom I had turned away at the chapel doors earlier in the day. They came with abominable witchcraft, religion and vile behavior, holding no invitations, dressed with no respect to the occasion. Pretenders. They shouted at the bride through that open window about how she could love the Groom and still go with them. "You don't have to go into the ceremony," they told her.

I kept thinking that if she would just move away from the window, if she would just take a single step toward the ceremony, I could fix it. However, the bride apparently was quite entertained, and as I looked at the situation, I felt I had lost her already. I closed the window, but it had little effect.

I still tried to prepare her for the ceremony. Getting her ready had become a massive chore. Then, she broke free from me. She pushed me out of the way and flung that door open. She ran through that large glass door at the side of the room like she was afraid of missing a bus, blocking it shut as she went.

The five angry, rejected wedding guests who had been dancing at the window earlier had beckoned to her, and she obliged them, drunk as they were. I was shocked at the speed and ease with which she went.

The bride might imagine that she was in control, but she was not in control of anything at all. She just gave her control, every ounce of it, over to the ones who were pulling her away from her Groom. She was quickly becoming their slave. She had forsaken the protection and covering of the King.

These five women were motivated by anger at what they could not have, at what they refused to pay a price to receive. They were hungry to take the bride's reward away, and she folded to their attentions, false hope and compliments. They became an uninhibited horde and surrounded her.

The level of excellence that was to be held within a relationship to the royal family would never be theirs because they were self-willed and disobedient to His heart. They refused, and here they were still refusing. They were jealous of the bride's love for the King's Son and of His love for her. They set out to destroy that love, all the while howling how they knew the King. Sadly, He did not recognize them.

I wished she would at least honor her gown and leave it behind, but she didn't. Instead, she disgraced the purpose of it. I ran after her and pleaded with her. "Please come back!" Violently, she threw me aside.

I knew by instinct and by experience that there was not much else I could do; she would not be forced. I have come to learn that sometimes you have to "cause" a person to obey and see the light. What I did not know then, I found out later. That day I was leaning on my own understanding. The day would come when I would lean upon the King's.

I watched from the door as the bride tripped over her gown, dragging it into the mud and mire, dancing with her tormentors and playing with pigs. The very gown of redemption and honor appeared to be a chain around her neck, an instrument of inconvenience, but she didn't take it off. She just drug it with her, fiercely and painfully, yet without a tear in her eye. Compromise had won the day.

I screamed with everything I had: "Don't go! It. Is. A trap. *Please*." I shouted again, "Come back!" She didn't even turn around. Eventually she tore her wedding gown off in the distance while she was being amused in the mud and put on clothing—ugly and seductive—from these women. She seemed to be drowning in her own selfish desires.

I ran after her and found the gown, and as I collapsed upon the ground to gather it up, I wept. I wondered how deeply the heart of this kind and generous King would break as He gave His beloved Son over to an ungrateful, unwilling disaster. The Groom, just days before, had been admiring His lovely bride who seemed to have eyes only for Him, and I wondered how long He would wait.

The bride was gone, having made up her mind with her distracted, now wicked, desires. She ran with her "new friends," and the thought of it made me sick. The sight of it made me angry.

They all ran into the dim light of the sunset, having no light to guide them, for the lamps they carried had no oil.

I could hear the wedding march off in the distance as if from a land across the seas of time, surreal and even mysterious in its cadence. And I wondered how long it would play.

As I reentered the chapel, the King tilted His head in pain, and I heard Revelation 22:11–12 echoing down the hallway: *"He that is unjust, let him be unjust still; and he which is filthy, let him be filthy still: and he that is righteous, let him be righteous still; and he that is holy, let him be holy still. And, behold, I come quickly; and my reward is with me, to give every man according as his work shall be"* (KJV).

The Groom never, ever, not once, took His eyes off the door where the bride was to emerge from. With a tear in His eye, He seemed to be praying for her return. Standing in between the door and the King, hoping and waiting. Interceding. The people in the chapel thought they were waiting on the King to begin the ceremony, but in fact, it was the Groom who was waiting on His bride.

I got busy "herding cats" and "managing fools," hoping and praying for a miracle. The people waiting for the ceremony seemed unbothered at the agony of the King and His Son. They were playing idiotic games and had become heavily distracted. I needed help but didn't know how to get it.

I gained my nerve and asked the King the question that was burning inside me. "Will the bride return?" I thought His answer would be thunderous, but it was a whisper coming from a cracked voice, almost broken. He said, *"It depends on how far she is willing to separate herself from the world."*

Then the thing that ruined me happened. The Groom began to weep, to fully sob; the King put His hand on His Son's shoulder as if to steady Him, yet the Son never took His eyes off that chapel door as He waited and waited. He was glorious in the midst of His broken heart. My soul ached for Him.

Then the King stood straight and shouted, "Send in the Herald." One who was battle-worn but not weary arrived with speed at the bidding of the King, ready to serve, anxious to please. I stood still, knowing this was the help I was waiting for.

The Herald marched about the chapel, taking no prisoners, making no friends. He was ready to uncover the cause of this defeat, and nobody seemed safe, for he would find the truth and devour it as medicine for the nations. He understood his mission with a piercing clarity and would not be distracted.

And there it was: a small creature in the corner, left unattended. A simple thing, really; quite unassuming yet not without blame. It had been whispering terrible things about the Kingdom that the bride would come to rule. It had instilled doubt in everyone in the room and fear in the bride herself.

It occurred to me that those who did not know the Groom should not have been in the chapel anyway. Bystanders, but not innocent. Those who knew the Son were the ones who would joy in the wedding, not others.

The Herald destroyed this creature while others screamed about how cruel and insensitive he was. The room cleared out, for they all had their part in what had happened. The Herald knew his job was to find the bride and restore her. But all along, he also knew that for some, when they have tasted evil, will refuse to return no matter how deeply the King calls or the Son weeps over them. (See 2 Peter 3 and Hebrews 6.) This knowing seemed to fuel his intensity.

As he spoke, there was a righteous indignation that came over him. I saw it like a vapor, like a smoke. In every move he made, in everything he said from that point on, there was a passion in him I had never seen before. I pitied the person who got in his way!

The Herald left the building and went on a hunt for the bride—marching, shouting and pronouncing the love of the King for her, along with the sacrifice and adoration of the Son. He knew that such kindness should have power over the evil that had overcome the bride. (See Romans 2:4.) His steps were well-ordered and fixated on his task. He was not going to lose.

The Herald did not stop; he ran with force into the restless night, determined to succeed. The King watched and His Son maintained His position of waiting at the door where the bride was to emerge from. His heart was so broken, I had to look away.

Then I remembered Matthew 24:24, how it said that if it were possible, the very elect would be deceived, and I wondered....

Time passed: two days, maybe three. The very earth was shaking, and the skies were rolling as the Herald maintained his rampage against wickedness.

The bystanders were gone. The chapel felt redeemed somehow, beyond a building. It was glorious. The King would not leave the platform, and His Son would not leave His position standing between the King and the door.

I had no idea, absolutely no idea, what I was supposed to do. So, I cried. First I cried out of frustration, then out of sorrow. There was nothing left to do as the Groom was in deep anguish over His beloved.

I was tired; I was hungry; I was thirsty...I was many things. The Groom was not. He was steadfast and focused like nothing I had ever seen. He refused to give up. He wouldn't. I am ashamed to say that I tried to make Him go rest, maybe eat a bit. He wouldn't listen to me. He was incredibly focused, and I think that, in my efforts, I simply became a potential distraction. I had not fully understood the scope of the situation yet, but I would. God help me.

I heard a distant cry from across the valley. A very loud whimper that seemed like it really should have been a whisper, but it was forced from the soul.

The Herald had gone beyond the mountain range on the other side of the valley, and this was where the noise was coming from. The mountains were on fire; they were melting like wax. The ground had split, and the sky was thundering. Lightning had caught the trees on fire and were continuing to strike everything in sight. The Herald ran right through it. It seemed like he caused all the fuss and destruction, but I couldn't be sure. He was invincible in his quest for the King.

Somehow the Herald looked about fifteen feet tall, even in the distance, which baffled me, but not for long. He had gained strength through the Word of God that he was shouting. He was getting stronger and stronger. He was emerging through the flames and smoke. The lightning didn't dare touch him. I was looking at a war zone, a terrible war zone. I then began to understand, just for a minute, the lengths that this King would go to for His Son and His bride. He wasn't going to go quietly into the night.

The Herald found the bride. I should have been happy, but I was so mad at her that a self-righteous anger came upon me. Even after I confessed this anger and tried to repent, I was still mad at her. I couldn't shake it.

I thought she would be fighting and screaming, but the noise I heard from her was a heart-wrenching whimper of sorrow and remorse. She didn't want to escape. She was speaking broken words with a terrified heart: "I have redemption through His blood for the forgiveness of my sin...."

I wanted to leave. She made me sick. I tried to leave, but the King said to me, "My Son became a curse for this cause, and if you leave and refuse to help, you have become worse that she who ran away."

I cannot put into words the tumbling thoughts that were living in me at that time. Then I knew why I couldn't shake the anger; it was because I, myself, had become part of the anger and in my self-righteous horror was calling that anger good and just.

Then I heard the Groom, as He then had His hands upon the door she was to enter from, weeping out words, "I have blotted out, as a thick cloud, your transgressions, and as a cloud, your sins. *Return to Me*, for I have redeemed you. I am holy and have commanded My covenant upon you forever."

I was thrown into this drama somehow—laying blame, hating the cheating bride, breaking for the King and His Son, and holding tight to my convictions that she wasn't worth it. What an incredible mess she created. I was perfectly fine before, just holding my position to get her ready.

Then it dawned on me...*I* was supposed to get her ready, and I failed. She didn't get away; she got away from *me*! I wept with deep sorrow, and I don't think I had ever felt that bad before. I curled up in a ball, just absolutely heart-struck. The King told me that I was as bad as that, which I hate, because I had no redemption in my heart.

I was forlorn and felt forsaken. Then I realized that I had forsaken myself and my beliefs. I was surely the predator I had not known.

I was howling like a wounded animal. I was forced to face my ugliness. How I loved the King and His Son, the precious Groom, but it was a lie because I was full of hatred and judgment. I screamed and cried for what felt like eternity. Such a wretch.

The room grew silent. I didn't have any tears left. There was a holy hush that came up from the floor and down from the sky all at the same time.

I heard the Herald shouting, and apparently, he is shouting at the bride: "Your Groom has commendeth His love toward you, in that while you were a sinner in sin, He gave His life for you. Stop grieving and be joyful, for He has shown you great mercy and redemption. He has given you a free gift, a wedding gift, and we will collect this great gift today."

The Herald carried the bride to the glass door that she originally ran away through. The Herald does not knock or ask permission to enter; he kicks out the glass and half the wall. The door goes flying across the room and slams against the entry to the chapel.

The bride was begging to be freed from the Herald so she could run to her Groom. He refused her and blocked the way. "No, go get ready," he told her, and then he gave me a sideways look. I thought it was because I looked so horrible with all the crying, then I realized it was because I *was* so horrible.

The Herald set her in front of me and said, "He gave Himself for us all that He might redeem us from iniquity to be purified unto Himself and called a peculiar people, zealous to do good works. You," he looked straight at me, "be peculiar and zealous and don't be slack again. I am watching like a watchman on the wall, a diplomat for the King. Cursing or blessing, you choose, and I will gladly enforce it."

I was trembling with the awareness of my error. I apologized to the bride. "I am so sorry. I should have watched you more closely. I should have destroyed those women who were calling you away when they were at the window. I should have been fierce and ferocious to protect you, whether you wanted it or not, I should have ....."

It was my one job, and I failed. It doesn't matter if the bride was getting mad at me or overpowering me. I should have figured it out and, basically, cared more. What a self-righteous train wreck I was.

I tried to apologize to the Herald as well, but he told me to be quiet and stop being full of pride. He said, "I do not need your apology; the King does. Apologizing to me only reinforces your pride, knowing that you have made an attempt at humility that you do not possess." I couldn't win. Then it dawned on me that my redemption in all of this was going to be hard fought, and that was okay.

I realized that this was one reason the Herald was the Herald. He was keeping things clean unto God and catching error, no matter how small. He was commanding the very air to worship the King in purity and holiness. It appeared that he would attack anyone, with no remorse, who dared bring trouble to the King. He was doing his job.

When I took ownership of my error and sin of judgment, I no longer hated the bride; instead, I rejoiced with her. I was madly in love with this one who had captured the Groom's heart, the one whom He adored.

The Herald brought in a new dress. I cleaned up the bride and washed her hair. I stitched up her wounds and ministered to her broken heart and crushed soul. In all of this, her spirit was strong as it still belonged to her Groom, and that was incredibly beautiful.

I buckled at the chorus being sung in the background: *"He has shown you what is good. What does the Lord require of you? To do justice and to love kindness, and to walk humbly with your God. What you do for another, you have done unto Me."* This reality came

81

to destroy my hidden wickedness, and I could barely stand. I understood that He *is* enough, more than enough, and it undid me. The kindness and forgiveness of this King was tangible.

The bride steadied me, and with the most heartfelt two words I had ever heard, she said, "Thank you." And she meant it.

The tears from the Groom turned into magnificent piercing shouts of joy. Angels filled the chapel. I was clearly out of place, but somehow beautifully tolerated!

The Herald winked at me, and maybe he smiled. He marched the bride down the aisle; I guess he doesn't completely trust me yet, and I don't blame him. I wouldn't.

And... the wedding, it was glorious.

"If Jesus was willing to be beaten and tortured to gain the salvation of mankind, the least we can do is tell them about it."

—Evan Minton
A Hellacious Doctrine: A Defense of the Biblical Doctrine of Hell, 2017

References

Anderson, Gerald H., ed. *Biographical Dictionary of Christian Missions*. New York: Macmillan Library Reference, 1998.

St. Benedict. "The Reception of Visiting Monks." *The Rule of St. Benedict*. Sixth Century A.D.

Bennett, Roy T. *The Light in the Heart*. Self-published, 2016.

Bits & Pieces. January 9, 1992. Mark Brunner, "Just Something I Believed!" October 17, 2005. *Sermon Central* (website). https://sermoncentral.com/sermon-illustrations/22138/just-something-i-believed-10-17-05-that-by-mark-brunner. Accessed September 9, 2025.

Bloom, Jon. "How Satan Gets a Hold on You." *Desiring God* (website). May 17, 2018. https://www.desiringgod.org/articles/how-satan-gets-a-hold-on-you.

Bridges, Jerry. BrainyQuote (website). https://www.brainyquote.com/quotes/jerry_bridges_525927. Accessed September 18, 2025.

Carroll, Keith. "Who Did Calvary Really Seek to Reconcile?" *Relational Gospel* (blog). January 28, 2024. https://relationalgospel.com/blog/who-did-calvary-really-seek-to-reconcile/.

Fénelon, François. Letter XXX. *Spiritual Letters*. 1700s.

Fosdick, Harry Emerson. AZ Quotes (website). https://www.azquotes.com/quote/532442. Accessed September 18, 2025.

Graham, Billy. "Courage Quotes." Wesley Methodist Church Klang (website). January 21, 2012. https://www.klangwesley.com/courage-quotes.

Guyon, Madame Jeanne. #51. *Gems*. Late 1600s.

Havner, Vance. AZ Quotes (website). https://www.azquotes.com/quote/1187265. Accessed September 18, 2025.

"James Calvert of Fiji." The Museum of Methodism & John Wesley's House (website). https://wesleysheritage.org.uk/object/james-calvert-of-fiji/. Accessed September 3, 2025.

Jowett, John Henry. *"Come Ye Apart," Daily Exercises in Prayer and Devotion*. New York: Revell, 1920.

Jowett, John Henry. *The Whole Armour of God*. London: Hodder & Stoughton, 1916.

Judson, Edward. *Adoniram Judson: A Biography*. 1883.

à Kempis, Thomas. *The Imitation of Christ*. 1450.

Langley, Kenneth. Chapter 3, "Theocentric View." Scott M. Gibson and Matthew D. Kim, eds. *Homiletics and Hermeneutics*. Grand Rapids, Michigan: Baker Academic, 2018.

Manning, Brennan. *Abba's Child: The Cry of the Heart for Intimate Belonging.* Colorado Springs, Colorado: NavPress Publishing Group, 1994.

Mattson, Carlene. Focus on the Family. April 1993.

Merriam-Webster.com Dictionary. https://www.merriam-webster.com/dictionary. Accessed September 5, 2025.

Minton, Evan. *A Hellacious Doctrine: A Defense of the Biblical Doctrine of Hell.* Self-published, 2017.

Penn-Lewis, Jessie, with Evan Roberts. *War on the Saints.* London: Marshall Brothers, 1912.

Querin, Donny. Personal letter. 2010.

Radmacher, Mary Anne. *Courage Doesn't Always Roar: And Sometimes It Does, Re-defining Courage with Daily Inspirations.* Newbury Port, Massachusetts: Conari Press, 2022.

Ravenhill, Leonard. *Revival God's Way.* Last Days Ministries, 1984.

Reynoso, Cynthia Querin. Personal letter. 2025.

Richter, Curt P. "On the Phenomenon of Sudden Death in Animals and Man." *Psychosomatic Medicine. May-June 1957; 19(3)*, 191-198.

Robinson, Darrell W. *People Sharing Jesus.* Nashville: Thomas Nelson Publishers, 1995.

Swindoll, Charles. *Living Above the Level of Mediocrity.* Waco, Texas: Word Books, 1987.

Taylor, J. Hudson. *China's Spiritual Need and Claim.* London: Hutchings & Crowsley, 1885.

Today in the Word. Moody Bible Institute. February 17, 1993.

Tozer, A. W. *The Divine Conquest.* Harrisburg, Pennsylvania: Christian Publications, Inc., 1950.

Washer, Paul. QuoteFancy (website). https://quotefancy.com/quote/1620355/Paul-Washer-A-lot-of-people-think-that-Christianity-is-you-doing-all-the-righteous-things. Accessed September 18, 2025.

"We Died Before We Came Here." Ministry 127.com. https://ministry127.com/resources/illustration/we-died-before-we-came-here! Accessed September 3, 2025.

Yancey, Phillip. *What's So Amazing About Grace.* Grand Rapids, Michigan: Zondervan, 1997.

Suggested reading to further your spiritual growth and stability: *Open Doors* by Caryn Ann Kilgore (Orison Publishers, Inc.).

About the Author

Sandra Hardister Querin was called at the age of nine to "prepare for the day" when she would preach the Good News. Although hampered by cystic fibrosis and it's complications for thirty years, she pursued the call of God and her education, holding an MBA, JD, MDiv and ThD. She married her high school sweetheart and was married for forty-five years. Sandi worked as a college professor and corporate executive as well as serving on staff of several churches until the Lord called her into full-time ministry.

She has been supernaturally healed of her disease and walks in miraculous healing power. Her ministry encompasses the heart of Christ and is predominately prophetic. The cry of her heart is for the lost to be saved and for the saved to be empowered by Jesus Christ.

Sandi travels the world spreading the gospel and bringing hope to the hurting, healing to the broken, and deliverance to all those who embrace the cross of Christ. The sick come to her meetings for their miracles and are not disappointed because Jesus does not disappoint. Sandi serves as a leader at The Revival Center in Clovis, California. To follow the services online or to find out more about Sandi and her ministry, go to www.abbasheart.com.

She enjoys her children, grandchildren, the many adventures her friends take her on when she is not traveling and serves as a Fresno County chaplain.

To reach Sandi, write or call:
1516 Draper Street
Kingsburg, CA 93631
559.897.9575

Or view her YouTube channel: The Revival Center, Clovis, California.

www.ingramcontent.com/pod-product-compliance
Lightning Source LLC
Chambersburg PA
CBHW061707120626
46550CB00003B/1130